History, Memory, Fiction

History, Memory, Fiction

New Dimensions in Contemporary Pakistani and Kashmiri Writing

DAVID WATERMAN

OXFORD
UNIVERSITY PRESS

Oxford University Press is a department of the University of Oxford.
It furthers the University's objective of excellence in research, scholarship,
and education by publishing worldwide. Oxford is a registered trade mark of
Oxford University Press in the UK and in certain other countries

Published in Pakistan by
Oxford University Press
No. 38, Sector 15, Korangi Industrial Area,
PO Box 8214, Karachi-74900, Pakistan

© Oxford University Press 2023

The moral rights of the author have been asserted

First Edition published in 2023

All rights reserved. No part of this publication may be reproduced, stored in a retrieval system, or transmitted, in any form or by any means, without the prior permission in writing of Oxford University Press, or as expressly permitted by law, by licence, or under terms agreed with the appropriate reprographics rights organization. Enquiries concerning reproduction outside the scope of the above should be sent to the Rights Department, Oxford University Press, at the address above

You must not circulate this work in any other form
and you must impose this same condition on any acquirer

ISBN 978-0-19-070882-5

Typeset in Minion Pro
Printed on 80gsm Offset Paper

Printed by MAS Printers, Karachi

Acknowledgements

COVER: *People walking in the sci-fi city at night* © Tithi Luadthong / Shutterstock

There is only looking, and finally seeing, what was always there.
Daniel Mendelsohn

*Don't turn your head. Keep looking at the bandaged place.
That's where the light enters you.*
Rumi

Literature [is] a source for truth when History fails us.
Hadil Karkar

Contents

Foreword	ix
Acknowledgements	xi
Introduction	1

Part 1 | Kashmir   11

1. TRAUMATIC EXPERIENCE, CRISIS OF SURVIVAL, AND HEALING   13
   The Exchange of Interconnected Histories in Soniah Kamal's *An Isolated Incident*

2. 'NOW AND THEN'   25
   Mirza Waheed's *The Collaborator* and the Contested History of a Place

Part 2 | The Personal is Political   35

3. MIGRATION, EXCLUSION, AND THE ENEMY WITHIN   37
   Personal and Political Displacement in Rafia Zakaria's *The Upstairs Wife*

4. LIFE-WRITING AND CULTURAL MEMORY   45
   Basharat Peer's *Curfewed Night: A Frontline Memoir of Life, Love, and War in Kashmir*

5. NEOLIBERAL 'SELF-HELP' AND WATER RESOURCES   59
   Mohsin Hamid's *How to Get Filthy Rich in Rising Asia*

Part 3 | War   71

6. PAKISTAN DURING THE AFGHAN WAR   73
   History, Legacy, and Contemporary Literary Representations

7. CULTURAL UNDERSTANDING AS MILITARY STRATEGY   85
   Mapping the Human Terrain in Nadeem Aslam's
   The Wasted Vigil

8. HISTORIOGRAPHY AND THE QUESTION OF   96
   'WHAT HAPPENED?'
   Uzma Aslam Khan's *The Miraculous True History of Nomi Ali*

Part 4 | Migration   109

9. EXIT WEST   111
   The Making of a World

10. SNUFFING OUT THE MOON   120
    Kino/Bio Politics, Movement, and the State of Exception

11. 'EVENTFUL' HISTORY, MOVEMENT, AND   134
    SOCIAL MUTATION
    Possible Futures

Works Cited   140
Copyright Acknowledgements   149
Index   151

Foreword

Since time immemorial, the history of mankind has been forged by migration and exploration, conflict, change, and adaptation. As David Waterman observes 'People have always been on the move, and history seems to be driven by movement'. The literary imagination, however, is able to address the unspoken or forgotten and provide new insights into history by creating a narrative which links the personal and the public, moving beyond the interpretation of facts to address the human experience and ferret out significant elisions. In doing so, literature can illuminate the historical narrative to create an understanding of the past, so necessary to our comprehension of the world we inhabit today, and the choices necessary to forge a better future.

David Waterman's incisive book *History, Memory, Fiction: New Dimensions in Contemporary Pakistani and Kashmiri Writing* sets out to explore eight contemporary written works, including both fiction and memoirs. He points out that 'even the most realistic of memoirs will also contain fictional elements as inferences and interpretations, filling in the gaps when memory fails.' As such, these books employ literature to describe historical events, including different forms of conflict, migration, and movement in the sub-continent.

History, Memory, Fiction is grouped into four sections. 'Part 1: Kashmir' looks at two novels that recreate troubled Kashmir; 'Part 2: The Personal is Political' examines three books, all of which link a historical trajectory with the pressures of daily life, including different forms of exclusion and 'migration'; and 'Part 3: War' begins with a discussion on the Pakistan-Afghanistan engagement and the American role. The second book recreates the brutal and forgotten stories of the Second World War in the Andaman Islands during the British and Japanese occupations. 'Part 4: Migration' explores movement, change, and globalization in two books; the first book traverses many countries, the second, several civilizations in the land which is now Pakistan.

Waterman's thought-provoking analyses of these texts is a welcome addition to his critical study *Where Worlds Collide: Pakistani Fiction in the New Millennium* (2015), which interpreted Pakistan with a chapter each on nine contemporary novels. His experience of Pakistan, together with his academic writings in French and in English on literary representations in international literature of war and conflict, give his work a universalism far beyond the subcontinent, with resonances in his recent work *Literature, Narrative and Trauma*, which he has co-edited with Aylin Atilla and Carlos A. Sanz Mingo (2019). The decision to include two Kashmiri writers of Indian origin alongside Pakistani writers is very important: the exploration of their writings on Kashmir, where they grew up, presents a daily reality beyond the usual 'condensed' geo-political tale and the political rhetoric of India and Pakistan.

In *History, Memory, Fiction*, the novels and creative memoirs that Waterman discusses are rooted in facts, but they explore the spaces in between, the 'possible worlds' which create a veracity that throw a new light on historical events. In other words, Waterman's analysis looks at the way in which imagination and storytelling, including the use of symbolism, metaphor, and the surreal, can reveal how political events and conflict impact nations and their citizens beyond selective ideological or political narratives, stereotypes, and perceptions. He covers many topical, political, and universal issues today, including geopolitics, the quest for a better life, and the ecological threats. Furthermore, all the books he discusses are works of some excellence.

History, Memory, Fiction is a thought-provoking book which explores some of the most important and topical issues today: the inequality of nations; ecological threats; conflicts in Kashmir, Afghanistan, and Pakistan, among others; and the migration from troubled homelands to foreign countries. The book also gives a rare account of little-known histories, which open out new horizons and paradigms, and highlights the diversity of Pakistani English literature as well.

Muneeza Shamsie
Karachi
May 2021

Acknowledgements

In spite of the many solitary hours of reading, note-taking and writing, producing a book is always a collective project, and I owe a debt of gratitude to many people for their comments, insights, and support. For the past twenty-five years, La Rochelle University on the west coast of France has been my academic home and paid me a salary for doing things I would probably be doing anyway. My research laboratories have provided funding for various trips to Pakistan, so that I was able to meet many of the writers, historians, politicians, activists, teachers and students, and thus I was able to benefit from their wisdom; many thanks to the Center for Research in International and Atlantic History and my new laboratory, Asian Dynamics, Interactions and Interculturality, in tandem with the wonderful colleagues at the University of Bordeaux Montaigne. As always, our International Relations service at the university has been a great help over the years in dealing with administrative hurdles: Stéphane Aymard, Isabelle Marchesseau, Isabelle Duhamel. When I am in Karachi the Beach Luxury Hotel has become my home away from home, and I could say the same for Islamia University when I am in Bahawalpur, for all of their legendary Pakistani hospitality. The Embassy of France in Islamabad and the various Alliances Françaises in Pakistan have always offered their support and encouragement, as has Oxford University Press in Karachi. Muneeza Shamsie has been my invaluable resource person for a long time now, and her generosity is boundless; Muneeza knows everyone, and everyone knows Muneeza, so I am always connected to the Pakistan network through her, and it would not be an exaggeration to say that much of my work would not have been possible without her guidance. In France, Paul Veyret of Bordeaux Montaigne University is my touchstone for sharing ideas on all things Pakistani, most often accompanied by an amusing anecdote about our experiences in the Land of the Pure.

Current and former PhD students from Pakistan, Syeda Sughra Naqvi and Raheen Fatimah Khan, have offered finer points of history and politics that only a native could provide, and finally to Dewi, who didn't think it at all unusual that I suggested bringing her to Pakistan for our honeymoon.

Introduction

In her essential and encyclopedic reference work, *Hybrid Tapestries: The Development of Pakistani Literature in English*, Muneeza Shamsie reserves well over one hundred pages for the Pakistani Anglophone novel, saying, 'By the dawn of the 21st century, Pakistani-English literature had started to come into its own and the Pakistani-English novel was in the vanguard of this international success' (382). Numerous pages of *Hybrid Tapestries* are also dedicated to the memoir form, an important genre in terms of cultural memory. The Anglophone literature of Pakistan, fiction or non-fiction, has both a long and a short history: long, as a consequence of the British colonial project on the sub-continent, and short, given that Pakistan has only existed as an independent and separate nation for the past seventy-five years or so, and of course the status of Kashmir has been contested ever since.

Contemporary history in Pakistan and Kashmir has been extremely condensed—what Sewell has called 'eventful' history—having witnessed many profound historical events, hence there is no shortage of topics which demand attention. Issues of Partition and migration, the role of Islam in governance, wars with India and ultimately the secession of East Pakistan, nuclear weapons, the status of Kashmir, war in Afghanistan and the resulting 'war on terror'—these preoccupations with national security also compete for attention with more ordinary, everyday concerns among contemporary Pakistani and Kashmiri writers: education, health care, strong institutions which could guarantee democracy and equal treatment before the law, the role of women, solid economic foundations, the environment, and so on. The current generation of Pakistani and Kashmiri Anglophone writers has addressed all of these topics and more, and indeed gained international recognition not only due to their literary craft but also because many of these works have very important things to say about our world in terms of social critique. It is perhaps no coincidence that quite a few of these novelists and memoirists are also journalists, frequently publishing essays in major newspapers like *The New York Times*, *The Guardian*, and *Dawn*.

This volume proposes an examination of several contemporary novels and two memoirs, considering them as historical fiction: in other words, as works that are based on real-world facts, but which, as fiction, are able to go further in creating what have been called 'possible worlds', ultimately crafting plausible stories that might well be true stories. By blurring the frontier between history and fiction, unconstrained by concerns of referential 'truth', these novels and memoirs are able to provide us with fresh insights and moral orientations while suggesting that the past—which is not the same as history—must be given meaning in our present if we wish to create better possible futures.

While the past has certainly happened, how it is perceived and represented is another matter entirely, making it necessary to speak of the past in the plural, given Hayden White's reminder of 'the inherent freedom of every human community to choose its own past and thereby its present' (Robert Doran, Introduction to The Fiction of Narrative, xix). White argues that all history is ultimately a history of the present:

> 'Men seem to require an ordered past as much as they require an ordered present. They want to believe that what they have in fact created could not have been otherwise. And historians assure them that this was so; out of the chaos of individual choices, the historian finds the order that even the choosers could not have seen. As they are lived, then, historical systems seem to move forward, into the future; as conceived and justified, they appear to back into it. Our anxiety in the face of the unknown drives us to embrace the fiction that what we have chosen was necessary, given our past. But the historical, unlike the biological past, is not a given; it has to be constructed in the same way and in the same extent that we have to construct our sociocultural present.' (White, Fiction 135; original italics)

White goes on to warn us that while the construction of our own present may indeed seem like freedom, seeking justification in the past destroys that notion of free choice and makes our societies seem to have been determined to become what they are

(Ibid.). A society which makes certain choices regarding its past via historical traces, memory (and forgetfulness), myth, tradition, imagination, and so on, and then interprets the resulting present as historically determined, has already limited its movement in terms of possible futures (see Paul Ricoeur 15–33). Seen from this perspective, it becomes clear that our communities are not so much progressing toward the future; rather, the future comes toward us from all directions, including the past. Fortunately, revision of the past(s) can, and does, happen all the time; White contends that the historical past is 'a complex web of nothing but revisions' (Philosophy of History after Hayden White 213). Such revisions can be undertaken for good or for ill, as a function of what we see as the necessities of our present, a means of making the past useful and meaningful, and then hopefully opening up more possibilities for futures as they come our way. How those choices are made involves morality and ethics, as well as compromises between realism and idealism. The fact that those choices may evolve in light of new information and experience evokes Benedetto Croce's work against fascism and utopian ideas; as White summarizes: '[Croce's] works seek to show that it is possible to live a life that is both heroic and civilized, even in the absence of total knowledge or divine power. The very ambiguity of moral action frees us to change direction in the light of every new, qualifying experience, allowing us to live by an ethical ideal that is both self-assertive and self-critical' (White, Fiction 65). It is precisely the narrative turn in historical studies that encourages us to see history as historiography—in other words, as a story told from a certain perspective and imposing a certain interpretation, which then allows us to orient a reader morally and ethically, as a 'purely' historical account could not do; chronicles simply describe, whereas history is by necessity an interpretation, which can be used self-critically. It is this articulation between history, memory, and fiction that this volume hopes to exploit, suggesting that fictional accounts, like the historical record or individual and collective memories, consist 'of provisional truths, of fictive possibilities, of approximative realities' (White, Fiction 103). These aspects all come together in the pages that follow, examining novels and memoirs as historical fiction, as part and parcel of the historical archive, telling stories that could be true, thus creating possible worlds. These stories admit, of course, the possibility of other equally true accounts while simultaneously orienting the reader to a certain way of seeing the world, thereby serving as social critique. The novels and memoirs under consideration are thus presented as activist, engaged literatures performing social criticism, and with good reason. Much of history has been written to erase or minimize events in the actual past, whereas those primary works which follow encourage us to pursue what White, after Ricoeur, called a 'fully realized historical consciousness [... After] the end of metaphysics, history seemed to be the only thing 'we' had left on which to build an ethics of care [...] and a politics of responsibility' (White, Fiction 321). That may seem a big responsibility to place on the shoulders of novelists and memoirists writing historical fiction, yet none of those under discussion call for social revolution. Instead, they seek evolution as the only realistic way of trying to make our world a better place, promoting an ethics of awareness that allows for imagination.

The volume is divided into four parts, organized thematically though with much overlap between the sections, all coming together within the grey zone between history and fiction as concerns contemporary Pakistani and Kashmiri Anglophone novels and memoirs. All of the essays treat primary works which have something to say about the real world (that is, a world which predates the text which describes it), while simultaneously participating in world creation (or a world which comes into existence because a text creates it). Part 1 examines two novels centered on Kashmir, Soniah Kamal's An Isolated Incident and Mirza Waheed's The Collaborator. Kamal's novel is a transnational and intergenerational story of a family killed in the ongoing violence, while the surviving daughter Zari flees to relative safety to live with distant relatives in the United States, carrying all of her traumatic baggage with her. While there, she meets Billy, who has grown up hearing romanticized tales of heroic freedom fighters, including his own grandfather. Billy is determined to fight for Kashmir's cause as well, yet once there he quickly realizes that realities on the ground do not correspond to his conceptions of glory and honor. Kashmir's cause then becomes secondary as Billy concentrates simply on surviving. Like any historical archive, by necessity always incomplete, these traumatic experiences also cannot come together and make a more comprehensive, therapeutic story until they are brought out of isolation, shared between Zari and Billy. If a traumatic past can never be erased, perhaps it can at least be worked through, thus allowing the victims to incorporate that past into their own histories and, hopefully, move on.

Waheed's novel is set along the Line of Control in Indian-occupied Kashmir, also a story of freedom fighters and the trauma of war, with the Vale of Kashmir becoming a representation that is fictional yet firmly grounded in the historical and political materiality of this contested space. Although the valley is a no-man's land, largely forgotten by the rest of the world, The Collaborator fills in the blanks of the archive to provide details which then record the historical reality of this earthly paradise littered with dead bodies. The novel is presented in episodes as 'Now' and 'Then', highlighting the roles of history, geography, and traumatic experience, in which past and present are never quite distinct and prospects for a better possible world are bleak. Arundhati Roy tells us that fiction is not simply an appropriate form to analyze such a situation—it may well be the only form possible; 'Kashmir, whose truth can only be told in fiction [...] Because the story of Kashmir is not only a story about war and torture and rigged elections and human rights violations. It's a story about love and poetry, too. It cannot be flattened into news' (Waheed, Collaborator 188).

Part 2 then treats the grey zone between the personal and the political, examining one novel and two memoirs, since memory, like the historical record, is never complete, always containing only fragments and traces, and even the most realistic of memoirs will also contain fictional elements as inferences and interpretations, filling in the gaps when memory fails. The frontiers between history, fiction, and memory are permeable in several directions: 'Fact and fiction,' Roy reminds us, 'Are not converse. One is not necessarily truer than the other, more factual than the other, or even more real than the other' (79). Rafia Zakaria's *The Upstairs Wife: An Intimate History of Pakistan* is at once political and personal, blending historical events with more personal details regarding migration, ethnicity, and polygamy, especially focusing on the situation of women. Migration can be large-scale, as after Partition, with many Muslims moving from India to Karachi, whereas the distance for personal migration is not as great: a first wife moving upstairs to make room for the second. Migration then sets the stage for exclusion, whether as migrant or as woman, whether Benazir Bhutto or Hamida Bogra on the national stage or 'dirty' local women arrested for adultery under the Hudood Ordinances. *The Upstairs Wife* ties national history to the story of the family, asking us to question the basis for such exclusion and questioning whether such brutal methods of community cohesion, by declaring an enemy within the fabric of our families and societies, are indeed necessary or desirable. This is, what Roy calls 'fiction that attempts to recreate the universe of the familiar, but then makes visible what the Project of Unseeing seeks to conceal' (168).

Basharat Peer's *Curfewed Night: A Frontline Memoir of Life, Love and War in Kashmir* is also an excellent memoir which invites us to look more closely at the absurdities of the status quo, since a relatively simple change of historical direction—a possible future built on present-day reflection on the past—would alleviate much pain and suffering. Peer recalls life in Indian-occupied Kashmir in the 1980s and 1990s, a memoir of his generation's experience, going from idyllic to traumatic, and establishing a form of cultural memory which includes historical elements as well as personal details and emotions. He thus creates what Birgit Neumann has called 'fictions of memory' with the goal of constructing a 'usable past' on which to propose a better possible future, a future which approaches us from all directions, including the past. *Curfewed Night* is at once a genuine historical memoir and an ethically engaged project of world creation. The third essay in Part 2 looks at a very real historical phenomenon, the shortage of water in South Asia, especially due to Chinese dam-building projects, which threaten downriver supplies, since most of the rivers of South Asia locate their headwaters in Tibet, controlled by China. Mohsin Hamid's novel, *How to Get Filthy Rich in Rising Asia*, is a rags-to-riches story of a poor boy who becomes wealthy by following the neoliberal mantra of self-help, choosing bottled water as his 'product' for sale to those who can afford it, never mind that a natural resource like water should, in theory, belong to everyone and be shared fairly. His personal rise and fall become a microcosm, reflecting South Asia's large-scale situation in terms of economic rise at all costs—greed, corruption, environmental damage—with no thought of long-term consequences in human terms. Ultimately, the protagonist in Filthy Rich is glad to be rid of his fortune and re-establish priorities on a personal level, if only the political actors would follow suit.

As was mentioned, many profound and often traumatic historical events have informed Pakistan's/Kashmir's history since Partition and are subsequently treated by contemporary Anglophone writers. Part 3 begins with a description of two nearly concurrent events, the Soviet invasion of Afghanistan and the associated military regime of General Zia ul-Haq, which have had devastating effects on Pakistan's present generations and as such limit the possible futures which are available to these people. US, Iranian, and Saudi interests during the Afghan war would be furthered through financial support to Pakistan, creating an irregular force of mujahideen fighters combating the Soviets, but with untoward side effects: Pakistan became a base for the so-called War on Terror, with a corresponding rise in extreme violence and a Kalashnikov/heroin culture left in its wake. Zia, as a staunch US and Saudi ally, was able to remain in power for over ten years and used much of the funding to further his hardline Islamization of Pakistan, which has also left scars on Pakistani society today, not to mention an ongoing Sunni/Shia conflict. The essay concludes with a brief overview of some of the contemporary literary representations of the Afghan war and Zia legacies before turning to the next essay, a detailed account of the history/fiction articulation relating to US involvement in the war and its representation in Nadeem Aslam's *The Wasted Vigil*. In Afghanistan, the US Army had deployed Human Terrain Teams consisting of civilian social scientists, with the objective of mapping the human terrain in cultural terms, a counterinsurgency approach based on a more efficient control of the population through improved knowledge of the host culture. While presented as a way to better avoid conflict with the Afghans, the fact that social sciences research was being carried out in collaboration with the military has raised many deontological questions. *The Wasted Vigil*, set in Afghanistan, introduces characters who are active or former CIA agents, culturally sophisticated, with different approaches to how such knowledge is to be exploited and to what ends. As with most counterinsurgency operations, the battle is already lost from the beginning.

The third essay of Part 3 approaches Uzma Aslam Khan's latest novel, *The Miraculous True History of Nomi Ali*, through the lens of historiography while trying to answer the question, 'What happened?' Nomi Ali is a work of fiction, treating the subject of a British penal colony on the Andaman Islands during World War II. Free from the referential truth claims of 'pure' history, the book is well adapted to filling the gaps in purely historical accounts with elements that have gone missing from official records, and is ultimately able to provide a plausible, possible world, which might be more true than more 'factual' versions in providing a set of answers to the question of what happened. Khan's novel succeeds beautifully at creating a meaningful version of the past, hoping to recover a largely forgotten episode of colonial history and make it useful in the present, once again by blurring the boundaries between history and fiction.

Finally, Part 4 looks at the issue of migration. Mohsin Hamid's *Exit West* addresses forced migration on a global scale—people fleeing war, hardship, and economic ruin. The novel is a good example, among many others, of contemporary Pakistani Anglophone fiction moving from regional to world literature. In the novel, magical doorways are the passages to other worlds, and the constant movement of peoples across the globe sets up a more plural view of humanity, thus in the end creating a new, possible world through the constant arrival of newcomers. This world in transition creates some conflicts regarding who belongs and who doesn't, yet the novel, by telling a fictional story about a very real situation, is able to arrive at a possible world which might have been unimaginable in the recent past yet seems much less unimaginable now.

The final essay of this volume is centered on Osama Siddique's novel *Snuffing Out the Moon*, tracing migration in the Indus Valley over a period of four thousand years. People have always been on the move, and history seems to be driven by movement, whether caused by invasions, expulsions, desertion and so on. The migrant becomes the politicized figure of movement, with biopolitical techniques of social control often aimed at the migrant, such that the politics of movement becomes a fundamental element of biopolitics. Further, we see that social flows are often exploited by a dominant power as a means of declaring a state of emergency or a state of exception, creating human beings who are both within and outside the law. *Snuffing Out the Moon* focuses on several different episodes in the history of the Indus Valley. These include one in the future, a totalitarian society that discourages its citizens from consulting the historical archive: a warning of the consequences of not learning from our own histories, or of not making sense of the past in our present.

PART 1 | KASHMIR

1

Traumatic Experience, Crisis of Survival, and Healing

The Exchange of Interconnected Histories in Soniah Kamal's *An Isolated Incident*

Soniah Kamal's 2014 novel tells the story of Zari, a young wife-to-be, who must flee her native Kashmir in the wake of political terrorism that has killed her family and fiancé, leaving her to bear the psychological scars which make survival itself a constant struggle. Sent to America to live with relatives in an upscale suburb, Zari is displaced spatially and temporally, torn from her Kashmiri roots and haunted by the past—ghosts who ask: 'Why did you live and not I?' (Kamal 43). The Pakistani-American family also bears scars—corporeal and psychological—from the past in Kashmir. Their son Billy falls in love not only with Zari but with a romantic ideal, compelling him to go to Kashmir as a freedom fighter to follow in his grandfather's heroic footsteps and avenge Zari. But the silence with which the family surrounds these traumatic histories means that Billy and Zari have acquired only partial stories and half-truths, with many pieces of the puzzle missing. Psychic healing can only begin when they exchange their 'interconnected histories', when they are able to make another person's history speak and thus re-signify the perspective of the past as a way of illuminating the traumatic shadows which have obscured this family's narrative (Nadia Butt 15; Jopi Nyman 112). Only by coaxing incidents out of isolation can the gaps of the story be filled, at least partially, thus forming a more coherent, more complete narrative of the past as a foundation on which to construct a viable, if imperfect, future.

The central dramatic event of the novel is the murder of Zari's entire family, including her fiancé, although by whom is not clear, within the confused environment of the Kashmiri conflict: freedom fighters, the police, the army, pro-Pakistan, pro-India, all inspire fear, even those who are supposedly on 'our' side. Zari herself is wounded in the attack, yet her gunshot wound is almost an aside to what is considered the greater injury, the fact that she was raped by the assailants and hence is now 'damaged goods'. Traumatized psychologically, Zari is trapped in what Nadia Butt calls a 'static zone', wherein past and present run together (5); although the police will classify the attack as an isolated incident, the incursion of the political into the intimacy of family life makes it clear that, whatever we are told about home representing safety (Kamal 19; Nyman 24), connections between past and present, political and personal do not admit of incidents in isolation (Butt 2, 9). Indeed, the attack itself is preceded by a night-time visit by several thugs, assumed to be freedom fighters, terrifying the family, demanding food and shelter for the night, and the later fatal attack may well be in retaliation for the family's 'aid' to the enemy. After the first intrusion, there is a heated debate among the family members regarding the risks involved in remaining in Kashmir, although now, with her family and fiancé murdered, Zari has little choice but to leave for the USA, even though the host family is reticent to accept her presence; Zari finds herself adrift in society, in a situation similar to what Janine Altounian (in a discussion wherein she cites survivors of the Rwandan genocide) calls 'severed links', whether within the psychic economy, between generations or within the larger social environment:

> A girl or woman raped, tortured […]. She has disappeared from society because no one approaches her properly […]. She continues to wander in society […]although she would prefer to live in a hole […]. *Without a past, without a childhood, because uprooted*: the survivor has a problem of reintegration, she is without family, without shelter, without neighbours, without means. Everything

around her has become strange: the people, the houses, the lifestyles […] the social environment does not understand her, neither does she understand it […]. She does not have the time, the means, the heart, to cultivate social relations.' (Altounian *De la cure à l'écriture* 35 ; Speciosa Mukayiranga, 'Sentiments de rescapés,' in Catherine Coquio (dir.), *L'Histoire trouée. Négation et témoignage*, Nantes: L'Atalante, 2003. 776-783. My translation, original italics).

In a chapter entitled 'The Survivor's Paradox: Betray the Dead?', Elise Pestre argues that the goal of the exterminators is to block all efforts to maintain 'the symbolic continuity between the world of the dead and that of the living, by making the border between these two separate universes permeable. [The exterminators] prevent the living from burying their dead, who will remain phantoms, forever seeking a place. Not assimilated with the dead, all the while trying to free oneself from the influence of death, such is the survivor's paradox' (117; my translation). Hence, these same severed links among the living are reconnected between the living and the dead in more than a symbolic manner, and will literally haunt Zari as the ghosts who ask, '*How are you still alive?*' (40; original italics). Ghosts are, Butt reminds us, nothing more than 'presence[s] displaced in time' (7). These ghosts make Zari wonder if she is losing her mind, despite the fact that such haunting, such survivor's guilt, is frequent among victims of psychic trauma. As Altounian reminds us, '[Victims] survive, haunted by the extinguished links to parents, to their former country and to their broken dreams' (48; my translation); Pestre too, during her fieldwork, reports that traumatized refugees often fear that they are 'going crazy' (71), and, in the novel, Zari often needs to reassure herself that she is still connected to reality by inflicting pain on herself with a razor (55 et. al). As it turns out, Zari's forced emigration to a family of distant relatives whom she does not even know will ultimately serve as the foundation for her future, her arrival the catalyst which will expose, even provoke, other traumatic experiences across generations, all linked to Kashmir. Zari is not as alone as she'd thought. Billy's father, Amman, for example, was tortured as a boy in Kashmir for his father's activities in the independence movement, and still bears the scars, both literal and figurative (73); he had moved to America to escape his past. 'No past to weigh them down, only a future in which to plant the flags of their dreams, [... where] the burdens of the father were not the burdens of the son' (274–5). Not wishing to burden his own son with the reality of the past, Amman unwittingly contributes to Billy's idealization of the freedom fighters, initially remaining silent when Billy demands to know his own history (75), yet later yielding to Billy's entreaties, revealing the story of his torture (161–5). Determined to become a freedom fighter in his own right, Billy will leave home for Kashmir, fueled by his memories of his grandmother, Mauj jee, and her stories of heroic freedom fighters, as well as Billy's own experience as a small boy on a visit to Kashmir, caught by accident in a violent demonstration and tear-gassed (81). Once he is on the ground in Afghanistan/Pakistan, Billy quickly understands that the reality of the Kashmir conflict is quite different from his romantic ideals. His objective of Kashmiri independence devolves into just 'keeping sane and getting out alive' (248). While in training, he will survive the bombing of the camp by US forces, and later will be responsible for his mentor's death from a landmine (307), thus acquiring his own traumatic experiences and survivor's guilt. Upon his return, he will then be better equipped to open up a space of understanding with Zari, better able to relate to her pain and loss. He will become what Altounian calls the Other, who is able to hear the truth within a context of shared stories (*De la cure* 130).

Although Zari has indeed survived, as will Billy, survival itself becomes a crisis, a day-to-day negotiation between past and present, and a future which is by no means assured—what Nyman calls lives 'crippled by memories' (120):

> The deluge of memories that came with the words, the accents, and the inflections bridged gaps in time, space, minds, and hearts. It made the past palpable. Never mind that sanity said it was gone. She could shut her eyes and taste what had once been home. But, instead of comforting her, the memories increased her guilt at having stayed alive (100).

Even before his own experiences of death and duplicity, Billy will realize that the crisis of survival, with all its associated guilt, is shared by many others. Crossing into Afghanistan on his way to training camp, Billy reads a plaque commemorating Surgeon Bryden, the lone survivor of the British Expeditionary Forces holding Kabul, and makes the connection between this isolated incident and all the others:

> Billy had a vision of a man dazed by the unbelievable spectre of being the lone survivor; of a tall girl rocking her dead nephew in her arms and discovering that being the lone survivor was not a boon; of all the lone survivors of all the battles in the world cursing their luck at dodging death. For the next half an hour or so, until they arrived at the border town of Torkham, Billy tried to erase from his mind the haunting of lone survivors (212).

Like Zari, Billy too will worry about his own mental health later on; while escaping from the ruins of the bombed training camp, the group of stragglers discovers that the neighboring village, where some of the women did the camp's laundry, was also bombed by the Americans—like Zari's family, retaliation for having aided the enemy—and he sees a goat which survived the bombing:

> *Why me? Why did I survive when no one else did? Do I have a grand purpose in life? Am I the chosen one?* Billy shook his head. The goat had not been speaking. It had not. It was not suffering from survivor's guilt (296; original italics).

The assorted ghosts, visions, and nightmares from which Zari and Billy suffer are perhaps best symbolized in the novel by Zari's suitcase, filled with family memorabilia, a suitcase 'daring her to unpack, daring her to find space outside for the things within' (44); Zari is of course carrying much traumatic baggage with herself, and it is not until she unpacks her metaphorical baggage that the process of psychic healing can begin. Such unpacking does not depend solely on Zari, however; the rest of the family must do some unpacking of their own, as a means of what Altounian, citing René

Kaës, refers to as 'articulating the flow of individual histories with the flow of collective history' (Altounian 6; Kaës xv; my translation).

As has been said, the Nabi family moved to America as newlyweds to escape the past not only for themselves but also to ensure that their children would have a brighter future. With the best intentions, they try to erase the past and refuse to talk about it with their children, yet the past cannot simply be erased. As Freud insisted: 'Nothing which was formed in the life of the soul can disappear, [...] everything is conserved in one way or another and can reappear in special circumstances' (Freud 49; Pestre 88; my translation). When Mauj jee's letters arrive for Billy, his mother hides them, worrying that the idealized family history that Mauj jee presents—Dada as a heroic freedom fighter—will influence Billy's young, impressionable mind; when Billy discovers the letters, his parents dismiss her as a senile old woman in order to destroy her credibility. But Billy's father knows that the heroic tale is a lie, that Dada was in fact a mercenary who would torture, rape, and kill anyone for a price, and it is this revisionist history—what Pestre calls a kind of neo-reality, a 'construction' or 'composition' created in the interest of psychic survival (134)—of Dada as a hero which sustained Amman as a boy, and which fuels Billy's desire to follow in his footsteps. Billy is forever pestering his father, 'tell me my history' (75), but is told that it would not be good for him to hear. Zari's situation too is treated as something which should not be discussed; when she arrives, Mrs Nabi speaks to *Khala*, assuring her that all is well, yet, 'there was no mention of why Zari was here in the Nabis' house, under their roof, and Zari couldn't tell if this omission made her feel better or worse' (51). For his part, Billy would like to help but doesn't yet know how:

> [Billy] longed to ask her what exactly had happened. But, since shutting the door on his face the first day they'd met, they'd had no interaction, and he was hardly in a position to ask her about anything. The fact was that no one in his family knew how to *help* Zari, let alone know what to say to her, though they all had questions (59; original italics).

The most taboo subject of all is Zari's rape, concealed under a cloak of euphemisms in the belief that the best way to help Zari is to get her married off quickly to anyone who will have her. Zari has been reduced to what Pestre calls a 'poor, traumatized victim' and despite good intentions, her host family doesn't really know how to help someone who has experienced what no human being should have to experience, a fact which obviously disturbs Zari but disturbs her entourage as well, as they try to protect her from shame and humiliation (Pestre 289; Kamal 7). For the moment, Zari's experience remains 'untranslatable into the language of the civilized world, in other words uncontaminated [...] by the terrors of an inhumanity to which the phantoms of the past testify' (Altounian, *De la cure* 49; my translation). Even Fahad, the handsome boy from a wealthy family who proposes marriage to Zari, does not want her to speak of her traumatic past; when she makes an effort to do so, he threatens to withdraw his offer of marriage (319). Although psychic healing depends on the exchange of interconnected histories, the survivor's story is often met with incomprehension, sometimes even skepticism; when the narrator exceeds the bounds of what is 'politically audible', the story then becomes threatening to the larger group, disturbing because of its 'inexpressibility' (Pestre 67; 132).

In such a context of mutual incomprehension, the standard response is 'I'm sorry', qualified by Zari as 'the stupidest, most impotent word in any language', to which Billy replies 'But it's better than silence. Anything is better than silence, isn't it?' (111). Billy's departure to become a freedom fighter is at least partly an attempt to better understand Zari and to relate on a more profound level to her experience; in the novel, the metaphor for such interchange and desire to know the Other is the children's game 'Who is that, who am I, then tell me who are you?' (254), a game which highlights not only the exchange of interconnected histories but also replicates the sort of triangulation through which the 'validation of a history' operates from one generation to the next. According to Altounian (citing Dany-Robert Dufour):

> For the transmission of a history/story to be certain, it must in fact be *heard* by one person from another, *told* (translated...) by the

same, and *re-heard* by a third person [...] The notion of transmission of a history/story [...] implies a series of *three allocutions* (Altounian, *De la cure* 130-131; Dufour 157. My translation, original italics).

But, as Billy will discover, it is difficult to respond to these questions in the present when the past is not only shrouded in silence but, when elements of the family's history do become known, they have been embellished, exaggerated, even falsified, and as Southgate insists, falsifying the past results in a present which has also been falsified (121). In Pakistan, Billy is sheltered by Chacha, a pro-independence militant who, in a situation reminiscent of Zari's, is not at all happy to take him in, knowing that Billy's personal chapter of the collective history may disturb his own. Like many others, Chacha is entangled in the complex web of Kashmiri intrigue, and hesitates to take a position: 'As for me, *naa aaar naa paar*, I belong neither here nor there...' (352). Yet he decides to take Billy into his confidence and shows him the archive he has been keeping over the years, an archive which Chacha asks Billy to organize and edit:

> Chacha looked at the boy, his arms folded over his chest, the armour of the stubborn. He's seen the same posture and the same expression plenty of times—they were the stances of youth and of fools—once he'd been both himself and for what he was about to do, he was still very much a fool. But it seemed necessary to let this young man know that there were men like him who were recording their dead, wounded, missing, and captured amongst the pro-independence freedom fighters for the memorials that would be built once independence finally came (354).

This archive is new data as far as Billy is concerned, and history evolves when new data becomes available (Southgate 163). Indeed, a paradox of historical research is the fact that more information does not necessarily correspond to greater certainty about what 'really' happened; more information may instead bring about more questions as perspectives are multiplied. Going through the files, Billy comes across some who are related to those he had known in the training camp and, more significantly, he comes across the entry for his Dada, the man who he'd grown up worshipping as a heroic freedom fighter. Chacha, however, knew him personally and tells Billy: 'And this one [...] it was said he specialized in torturing children' (356). Billy is understandably overwhelmed, shocked by the realization that his grandfather, far from being a hero, was a mercenary criminal:

> His grandfather was a hired gun.
>
> His grandfather was known for torturing children.
>
> Mauj jee was either delusional or a bona fide liar.
>
> His father had lied to him.
>
> *He was a Nabi, it was in his blood.*
>
> His father had tried to protect him from the legacy of bad blood (357; original italics).

Chacha too is concerned with the sharing of histories, difficult though they may be to hear, although he is projecting even further into the future and laying the foundation for mutual understanding on a larger, more collective scale, if and when independence should occur. He is clearly interested in the moral and ethical value that his archive will contribute to collective history, as well as to history's 'vital *therapeutic* function', also on a collective scale (Southgate 168; original italics). On a personal level, Dada's legacy as a hero had been the one thing that Billy believed in, having made it clear several times that he did not believe in God. He is therefore understandably shattered, and has become, in his own way, damaged goods, because his history, his inheritance, has suddenly changed. Billy now has a choice to make: let the facts speak for themselves, as Chacha has done, or rewrite history so that the Nabi family can still boast of their heroic ancestor:

> [Billy] could give his father a gift. He could—Billy sank onto the floor—revise history, rewrite it, regenerate it into palatable fare. [...] Billy's portrait could dilute history here, embellish it there, play with truth, tryst with falsehood, select, erase, exaggerate, downplay,

simply recreate and change the very essence of who someone had been and in doing so change history itself; [...] In willfully creating a life of lies, would he be able to live with himself or did lies become one's own truth too? (357-8).

History is always only partial and always contains elements of fiction. Like a palimpsest, history is sometimes written over and often seems to be concealing something (Southgate 31, 140, 136). Billy, understanding this, could indeed rearrange the past, but if his objective is psychic healing for himself and for Zari, the past must be faced, owned and worked through, not concealed or sugarcoated, and certainly not eliminated—an impossible venture in any case. Billy's principal reason for coming to Kashmir in the first place has suddenly evaporated, yet his journey has been productive nevertheless, and in learning the truth about his Dada, he will return to his family a changed man precisely because he refuses to compromise with history: 'He was no longer the person who'd left the US, nor was he the person who had left the training camp. That Bilal was gone' (Kamal 358). Billy's past—his history—is still there, but it too is something else, having changed because his perception of it has evolved (Southgate 181).

And so, Billy decides to go home. He is one of the lucky ones who has survived, survivor's guilt notwithstanding—and can make the choice to leave. His notion of 'home' has evolved along the way and, while Kashmir will always remain a central element in Billy's conception of where he comes from, it will never again be considered 'home', although being 'unhomed' does not make Billy 'homeless' (Nyman 23). Ultimately, Billy's voyage has been successful, since he had to learn his own history—although, when history is 'so near to us that it hurts', it is not considered history—before being able to share it with Zari and his family (Southgate 118; Wyndham Lewis 118-119). Certain secrets had already come to light during Billy's absence, such as his marriage to Zari, and he now learns that she is pregnant as well (363). Once home, Billy and his father finally speak about Dada—the real Dada—Billy's father admitting: 'After his father died, Amman had resolved to never speak of his father again, but he had soon realized that he could just as well recreate the memory of this father into one that was palatable' (370). Billy too could have changed Dada's story, yet chose not to: 'I could have changed it … I could have rewritten who Dada was. I could have made him an honourable freedom fighter. But I didn't. I couldn't' (371). Zari too wants Billy to tell her everything; so he does (372), coming to a pessimistic, indeed cynical conclusion, yet much more realistic than his preceding romantic idealism:

> The greatest deception is reaching into history to crack the code of life, believing there are lessons to be learned, that they shall be applied, that our lives, lived in our own little times, will make a difference, always good of course, for the rest of time. Listen closely, there is no message, no saving grace, no balm that will outweigh a final blow: a smile is no different from a scream in the galaxy of indifference that is time (372).

Although he feels ashamed, considering himself a failure, Zari assures Billy that self-acceptance is a form of heroism too, as she comforts him and explains:

> The first time you laugh […] the laughter will be a vomit that *will* make you sick, but it's a purge, that laughter … a purge that empties out some grief so you can replace it with some little bit of joy (Kamal 373; original italics).

Zari is speaking from experience and, while the two of them—and their family—are well on the road to healing after having shared their stories and experiences and feelings, they worry too about the next generation, which stands to inherit traumatic experiences as they have. Sharing histories, after all, is not without risk, as Zari wonders about 'her duty to tell her child about its history? But what if she was asked: Why did you tell me about all this?' (284). Even so, silence is the greater risk; the crisis of survival only begins to improve when a space is opened up to share traumatic experiences, to narrate the history of what 'really' happened in spite of the pain, and to be willing to listen to others who have suffered what no human being should ever have to suffer. A victim can never be 'de-traumatized' (Pestre 257) yet, by revealing their 'shared heritage'

(Southgate 149), a heritage which can never be received passively, according to Altounian (*La survivance* 144; Kaës 197), this family is better able to construct a future which necessarily includes the catastrophic events but is no longer overwhelmed by them. Billy's first word to Zari after his return from Kashmir, as he pulls a cookie from his pocket, is: 'Share?' (365).

2

'Now and Then'

Mirza Waheed's *The Collaborator* and the Contested History of a Place

Mirza Waheed's 2011 novel is set in Kashmir, as the first page makes clear, with a map of the region including the Line of Control separating Indian from Pakistani-administered territories. Narrated by a village boy from an idyllic valley near the border, the collaborator of the title tells the past-and-present hi/story from his own perspective as the 'abandoned one, the left-out one, the one who must tell the story' (80), while all of his friends have left to become freedom fighters. *The Collaborator* lends itself to a geocritical approach, by definition interdisciplinary, which argues that lived experience, including identity formation, happens within a given place, and that the subjective/fictional representations of the novel are grounded in an underlying physical, historical and political materiality, what Eric Prieto calls an 'activist' approach to space (17):

> No matter what the starting point—whether psychological, social, identitarian, political, or environmental—and no matter how much of a tendency we have to forget this basic fact, human identity […] is inextricably bound up with the places in which we find ourselves and through which we move (18).

In contemporary Kashmir, it is not simply spatial geography which is contested, but the history of how it got that way over time—the 'Now' and 'Then' titles of chapters in the novel—in a region where past and present are not so easily separated, and the situation evolves rapidly. 'For Kashmir there is always an Indian and a Pakistani version of everything [...] In the border areas, you see, it was a very confusing time—we didn't know how things could change between today and tomorrow, between morning and evening' (Waheed 15; 27). Within the genre of the post-colonial historical/Partition novel, *The Collaborator* may be read as being among 'ethically engaged interpretations of the actual past—and, as such, a meaningful source of knowledge about the past [...] where divergent understandings of history threaten to split the imagined community' (Dalley 5). Traumatic experience too, as described in the novel, often impedes, indeed contests, a distinct separation of past from present. Hamish Dalley suggests that the allegorical realism of a novel like *The Collaborator* is specifically postcolonial as an ethically and politically motivated representation of 'places where memories of past violence fissure the imagined community, and, as such, become subject to contestation' (9-10). In a region where both India and Pakistan accuse each other of being occupiers, even the local village people are not considered Kashmiri, but recently-settled, nomadic Gujjars, hence lacking the credibility of grounded identity and needing ID cards issued by the authorities in order to justify their presence. Collective trauma especially destabilizes the community, and there is much that is not openly communicated among and between the villagers in the novel; silences abound— even the landscape is silent: 'The small birches on these downy mountain folds just don't talk' (80)—leaving those who remain with the task of interpreting what is left unsaid, of incorporating those gaps within the story that must be told.

The valley itself is described as idyllic, although the opposing Indian and Pakistani check-posts have been there for a long time, and have become part of the materiality of the landscape, almost overlooked, as the protagonist makes his way for the first time into the valley in his new role of collaborator, of corpse accountant:

> When I go down the first time after all these months, years, it is with a sense of both pressing nostalgia and fear. [...] It's still the same—a calm, largely uninhabited, solitary place nestled amidst the rings of our hills and mountains. In my childhood, it was very

easy to ignore the Pakistani and Indian check-posts on either side;
you forgot about them the moment you stepped on new, untouched,
fresh-from-dried-dew grass … (6-7).

The check-posts were there then, and they are still there now,
external forces acting on 'our' hills and mountains, but the landscape
in which young boys would improvise a cricket pitch and go
swimming in the river is now composed of dead bodies, not even
a graveyard but an open-air dump for corpses:

> I look at the first few corpses and am immediately horrified at the
> prospects of what my first ever job entails. […] Bodies after bodies—
> some huddled together, others forlorn and lonesome—in various stages
> of decay. Wretched human remains lie on the green grass like cracked
> toys. Teeth, shoes. For God knows how long I just cannot remove my
> eyes from this landscape, heaps of them, big and small, body parts,
> belongings littered amidst the rubble of legs and arms (7–8).

The landscape has become (in)human, the scenery literally
composed of the casualties of the ongoing war in Kashmir; as we will
see later on, the protagonist, wondering if he is losing his mind, will
quite literally interact with the landscape, speaking with it, seeing
ghosts, remarking on the cohabitation of corpses and yellow flowers
(150) in his valley, where the crows grow fat feeding on human flesh
(49). This landscape especially is not simply a product of nature,
but has been socially produced, as Prieto reminds us: 'Space is not a
neutral featureless void within which objects and events are situated
but a dimension that has been produced by social forces that in turn
constrain future possibilities' (17), a dimension which must include
history, or time and the social forces which drive history, within the
equation. Fiction, which is able to go beyond what is found in the
standard historical archive, becomes a tool to explore what Prieto
calls 'interstices', allowing 'new ways of seeing what we thought we
already knew, new tools for seeing what had remained unnoticed
because it was caught in the cracks between known entities' (20).
The valley becomes an allegory for such an in-between space, a
landscape composed of decaying corpses, yet which are not in fact

simply casualties of war. The valley itself is not the battleground but a showcase for propaganda that neither side is willing to record in the archive; it has been created, as the Captain explains to the protagonist, to be 'a slap in the Pakistani's fucking faces' (292). The Captain then goes into greater detail regarding the ultimate 'normality' of such a landscape, for everyone to see:

> I show them what happens to the boys they send across ever so readily. It's my way of telling them, look, here are the wretched remains of your proxy soldiers, here are the rosy Kashmiri boys you trained, here lie the dreams your motherfucking ISI weaves [...] It's our bloody answer to their fucking devious ways: *Look, look, you back-stabbing bastards, here's your fucking jihad in a hideous heap, look at it and squirm.* And they can't fucking do anything about it, you see, not a fucking fig! Because *what* will they say? [...] You see, by burying them somewhere secretly you're inviting scandal, you are inviting discovery, you're asking for an 'uncovering', you're making news ... But by leaving them like this, I have already made them acceptable, you see, it's all open, kind of common, maybe a bit ugly, but normal (293; original italics).

Bertrand Westphal, whose ground-breaking work, *Geocriticism: Real and Fictional Spaces*, has led the way in theorizing the referentiality of literature with relation to the real, insists:

> Fiction does not reproduce the real, but actualizes new virtualities that had remained unformulated, and that then go on to *interact* with the real according to the hypertextual logic of interfaces [...] fiction detects possibilities buried in the folds of the real, knowing that these folds have not been temporalized (171; original italics).

Although a work of fiction, *The Collaborator* brings new perspectives of 'real' historical events to the fore, and the valley, as an allegorical fold in the real, is now exposed to scrutiny and demands to be temporalized. In other words, it demands inclusion within history and the record of that history. The 'no-man's land', wherein 'what happens here is off the record, means nothing to anyone' is simply the protagonist justifying his target practice on cadavers, with his newly-acquired pistol. He has, in fact, placed his own actions on the record as well (98).

Geopolitics is a central element among the social forces which 'create' space and is important in any geocritical approach to the novel. Although the valley and the surrounding mountains are described as 'our land' (66), the ongoing conflict on the Line of Control means that those who live there have lost much of their agency, their lives and deaths decided by other actors in India and Pakistan, using military equipment supplied by China, causing the protagonist to remark, '... Beneath all the green is a crimson red' (47), green and red being the respective colors of Pakistan and China, or, on a metaphorical level, the verdant valley tainted with blood. In the changing world of politically-contested borders, this landscape has become known as the 'gateway of militancy' as politics has become violent and freedom fighters of diverse origins have taken up arms, as a drunken Captain Kadian explains to the protagonist:

> We don't ask their nationalities, man. We just gun them down. [...] Did you really think your damned valley would be full just from the machine-gun fire from the check-posts here? No sirrr, no! This camp was set up to check one of the biggest infiltration routes in all of Kashmir, you must remember—the militants had it easy till then, come and go, come and go, all the time, like a fucking picnic. They called it the fucking 'gateway of militancy'! Then I came and screwed them, I cloz-zed the gates, heh! (96).

Then, the valley was a temporary stop along the trail for nomadic Gujjars with no regard for borders or lines of control, but now the nomads have become sedentary, and those who engage in cross-border wandering are the enemy by definition, regardless of their origins or intentions, and are killed. The valley has not physically moved, yet its meaning has changed. The town too, called Nowgam, has evolved from a sleepy one-road village into a politically-charged military zone, the last town before the border wherein posters proclaiming *Azadi* [freedom] appear 'out of nowhere' (175) and at night boys chant slogans from the rooftops: 'The wave had swept all of Kashmir and finally reached our village, in some force, the forgotten last village before the border. Posters competed for space on the sparse street walls' (176), until finally the commandos arrive and enforce a strict curfew, day and night, a lockdown which even includes the landscape: 'The entire state, all of Kashmir, even the lakes and rivers and ponds and the floating gardens of the Dal Lake, had been under curfew ever since the new Governor had arrived' (177). The population of Nowgam has been dwindling, between the young boys who have left for Pakistan to become freedom fighters, and the extrajudicial executions of those suspected of being or aiding militants, including the muezzin; the town itself seems to focus on the protagonist, wondering what his role has been and why he is still with his headmaster's family when all of his friends have gone: 'Nowgam waited for me to leave' (109). In the current climate of tension and fear, the majority of villagers have lost all hope of remaining; after a town council meeting, a mass exodus is planned and the village is described as a living being: 'For a moment it looked as if the whole village were moving. It felt as if things had just lifted, unhinged from their mooring places, and acquired a will of their own. A dust was sweeping away the village' (250). The ultimate goal of the Indian authorities was exactly this, to almost, but not entirely, eradicate the village, as Kadian explains:

> And by the way, yes, we didn't want a hundred per cent exodus from your village, we wanted it to remain, at least on paper. You see, there's a ration supply still listed and active in the Food Fucking Corporation of India, and the development-shevelopment funds in the behanchod DC's office, and the damned last village before the LoC still exists, doesn't it? (294).

So, although hardly anyone lives there any more, Nowgam has not become a non-place, as it so easily could in a purely fictional, 'imagined space' reading of the novel. As Edward Casey argues, there are no 'genuine locations in imagined space [...] only transitory *locales*, which do not last from one imaginative presentation to another' (Casey 156; qtd. in Sten Pultz Moslund 40). When approaching a text geocritically, or as a representation of historical fiction, we must of course reject such a reading as precisely acontextual/ahistorical, as Moslund suggests:

> It is so easy from a placeless and disembodied imaginative point of view to speak of distribution and free cultural flows as the primary forces of the contemporary world while dispensing entirely with the friction of places and processes of human emplacement. Things become far more complex the moment we equip human beings with bodies and see the imagined dimensions of their cultures and transcultural processes as interacting with physical dimensions and local environs (40).

This space, these people's homes, their valley, and mountains have been evolving, and a geocritical approach allows us to examine that situation from multiple perspectives, as Robert T. Tally explains: 'explor[ing] the overlapping territories of actual, physical geography and an author's or character's cognitive mapping in the literary text' (Tally 4; qtd. in Peta Mitchell and Jane Stadler 54), which, as has been suggested, is one of fiction's advantages over official historical archives; Westphal then links this multiple approach to identity, in that a dialectical perspective 'confirm[s] that any cultural identity is only the result of incessant efforts of creation and re-creation', though perhaps not decided by the people themselves (Westphal 114; qtd. in Mitchell and Stadler 54).

Much has been changing in the valley, and the people have had to adjust to this 'new reality' (Waheed 77), and as a consequence their way of looking at themselves and others—their individual and collective identities—has been changing too; they are now part of the 'Kashmir problem' (229). As has been said, the Gujjars were a nomadic people, only recently settled, and now their valley has become strategically important. The headmaster reminisces, going back to his memories of Partition:

> The truth is that I had actually believed, quite naïvely I must say, that not many people from among us would want to join the Movement, and that no militant group, neither the Liberation Front nor the Hizb-ul-Mujahideen, and none of the grandly named latest ones either, would want to come here, because for most people Gujjars

were seen to be always on the move, shifting from place to place; and anyway, who would care about a small, secluded community living in this tiny, sparse hamlet hidden in the midst of the mighty hills near the border with Pakistan. So, I had thought (27).

As it turns out, not only are the militants and the Indian Army very active in Nowgam, but many of the young boys have left to join the ranks of freedom fighters. This community has become sedentary, without really having a choice, and has also been becoming more religious in this region where Sufi mysticism had been the norm, where there was no mosque in the village, and where no one understands Arabic:

> Now, everyone seemed to be in a rush to make up for a lifetime of lost blessings, to catch up with divinity. Very soon, and almost unheralded [...] sincere religious devotion became a priority occupation for many in the village [...] and soon, very soon, people's faces changed too (30).

After a particularly moving sermon by the Moulvi, warning against the path of *kufr*, 'the crowd fell silent with a reverence I had never seen before [...] Something new, strange, powerful was going to happen sometime soon—an unnamed dread had begun to settle down inside me' (32). Even the walls of the village must now share space with graffiti 'declaiming reminders to divine duty' (30) alongside posters demanding freedom. In terms of identity, the changing geography of the valley and the village have had an effect on the community, as Christine M. Battista, citing Foucault, explains, wherein geography 'enforced, in Foucault's terms, a degree of 'normality' that produces a 'homogeneous social body' not only at the 'level of consciousness' but also 'at the level of what makes possible the knowledge that is transformed into political investment' (Battista 115; Foucault 184–5). A landscape of corpses in the valley, political slogans chanted from rooftops and posted on walls, a newly-built mosque filled with the faithful come to hear sermons inciting toward action, this cultural and physical environment, this space where people live and work and get on with everyday life is what David Quammen has called 'matri[ces] for destiny' (Quammen 180, quoted in Westphal, xi), everyday lived experience of/in a space which then orients this community's movement in the future.

Dalley warns us that 'the postcolonial world is characterized as a space in which history can never be taken for granted, and is subject always to conflict over past events and their meaning for present generations' (4), the 'Now' and 'Then' in which history, geography and traumatic experience create a constellation in which past and present are never quite distinct in a contested Kashmir, and prospects for future progress are bleak. As a postcolonial historical novel, *The Collaborator* goes well beyond purely historical accounts and is able to narrate traumatic experience by grounding such experience in a certain time and place within a specific material reality which affects, and is affected by, those who live and die there. The resulting story then gains ethical and moral credibility by exploring what is generally left out of historical accounts: the hopes and fears, dreams and nightmares, loves and hatreds of the people who live in Kashmir as they negotiate their future as the contested place between India and Pakistan. *Azadi*, tragically, is a long way off.

PART 2 | THE PERSONAL IS POLITICAL

3

MIGRATION, EXCLUSION, AND THE ENEMY WITHIN

PERSONAL AND POLITICAL DISPLACEMENT IN RAFIA ZAKARIA'S *THE UPSTAIRS WIFE*

Although classed as 'Memoir/History' by the publisher, Rafia Zakaria's *The Upstairs Wife: An Intimate History of Pakistan* (2015) reads very much like a novel and, like much of contemporary Pakistani Anglophone fiction, this memoir weaves together the personal and the political, foregrounding the situation of women in both public and private lives. Migration is treated on the macro-level of Partition, creating the need for domicile certificates, yet the work also tells of personal migrations, bridal leave-takings and the upstairs wife of the title moving from one floor to another. Exclusion can be political, whether Benazir Bhutto's exile, Zia's laws to constrain women, or the fact that opportunity is often linked to ethnicity. Personal exclusion takes on the form of two wives sharing a husband, yet never in the same week. Underpinning these threads of migration and exclusion is the sentiment that there is an enemy within the fabric of society, in what Laurent Gayer calls the 'ordered disorder' of Karachi — refugees forming a fifth ethnicity, East Pakistanis desiring independence, terrorists on the run from the FBI, or, more intimately, Afghan squatters in the vacant lot next door, or the second wife who lives downstairs. Pakistan, founded as a homeland for South Asia's Muslims, also belongs, as Zakaria insists, to Muslim women. Overwhelming importance is accorded to the family in Pakistani fiction and memoir, both on a personal level and as a metaphor for the nation writ large. The story of the family is ultimately the story of Pakistan; the two cannot be separated and, given that much of contemporary Pakistani fiction is historical fiction, the family becomes the foundation on which the history of Pakistan is constructed, an articulation which Zakaria develops fully in her history/memoir *The Upstairs Wife*. She accomplishes what a purely historical account could not. According to Beverley Southgate: 'Professional historians may provide "a chart of the facts" that governed people's lives in the past, but such history "withholds the closest *human* things, the touches of *direct experience*' (Southgate 6; Southgate refers to an essay by Herbert Butterfield, 112; Southgate's italics). *The Upstairs Wife* thus evolves into something akin to what Horst Steinmetz calls 'something more than history' without becoming false (89). By working in the grey area between history, fiction, and personal experience, the author has greater latitude to address morality and ethics, or foreground minor characters as agents of history well beyond official accounts, or psychologize historical figures, for example, yet remains coherent with a reader's expectations of what such a possible world could or should be like. Beverly Southgate suggests that historical fiction's advantage is to raise questions, not only regarding what has been written into standardized versions of history but more importantly, what has been written out in terms of what 'really' happened, thus revealing the exploitation of 'history' as a political tool (159–60). It goes without saying that historical fiction and/or memoir become political tools in their own right by questioning such gaps, or by telling an alternative story, which indeed might be just as true as a purely historical account.

Pakistan was created amidst the greatest migration of human beings ever, a political leap of faith after years of militancy not only for independence but also for partition, resulting in ethnic tensions between natives and newcomers, as Roger Ballard suggests: 'Such conflicts have many dimensions, but the driving force behind racial and ethnic polarization is invariably to be found in competition for scarce resources. Hence tensions between 'natives' and 'immigrants' are invariably most acute during periods of recession; and they are most easily sustained where the newcomers are easily identifiable' (21). Those easily identifiable newcomers were called Muhajirs. While tensions had been simmering for some time—Nichola Khan tells us that the Karachi conflict of 1984–2002 'was dominated my MQM's involvement in intense violence' (6)—Zakaria highlights the well-known incident of Bushra Zaidi's death in 1985, a twenty-year-old Muhajir student killed as she crossed the street in front of her college; the bus was driven by a Pashtun, and enflamed passions along ethnic lines throughout Karachi:

> It was the beginning of an ethnic war that would outlive them all. In the days that followed, hundreds died, and from their blood a fifth ethnicity emerged in Pakistan. There were no longer Sindhis, Punjabis, Balochis, and Pashtuns, each neatly attached to a province in a country that then had four of them. This new ethnicity was called 'Muhajir', or 'refugee', an umbrella name for all those whose families migrated to Pakistan post-1947, all those who now lived in a Karachi straining at its seams (136).

But Zakaria doesn't stop at ethnicity within this political equation; she also makes it clear that the young women of Sir Syed College were also being targeted as women, as the police reaction to their public protest explicitly shows:

> The policemen didn't care. They grabbed and groped the girls, their breasts, faces, and hair, intent on teaching them a lesson. They were being taught not to leave the boundaries of their campus, not to ask for something the men did not want to give them; they were being taught the consequences for speaking up (135).

In a related vein, Kamila Shamsie points out that, at the time, Ziaul Haq underestimated the power of women in the public sphere. She uses the example of the Women's Action Forum, born in response to the Hudood Ordinances, whose demonstration in Lahore in 1983 against the Law of Evidence saw:

> hundreds of women protestors assaulted by the police [...] the women's movement showed how it was possible to launch such an

attack by revealing the hypocrisy at the core of so-called Islamization and raising the right to question interpretations of Islam (50).

The description of physical violence we see in *The Upstairs Wife* could very well be an historical account, an eyewitness rendering of the event itself (as unreliable as eyewitness recollections can be), yet the reader is also made privy to what the policemen were thinking at the time, the motivations which seem to guide their behavior, the kind of information which exceeds 'pure' history and which is generally not found in historical archives—exactly the kind of 'something more than history' which adds an ethical/political element to this event. Without such information, one could interpret the police repression simply as enforcing order when faced with unruly citizens; with this information, one understands that these protesting citizens are being targeted and attacked *because* they are women. Migration on the personal level is also a heavier burden for the women to carry, resulting in loneliness and the 'loss of the brood' (137):

> Surrayya discovered what would become the harshest revelation she would face as a migrant. The hours between her husband's departure for work and her children's return from school were empty. Days that had once seemed too short, crammed as they were with conversations over window ledges and stair landings, lay fallow and featureless. […] She did not yet know the rules of living among strangers in Karachi, and she did not yet guess that she would be, now and forever, surrounded by them (47–8).

Even Aunt Amina's 'migration' to the third floor, a distance of only a few steps, is significant, since 'heavy curtains and solidly built subterfuges can make denial a possibility' (151).

Migration can lead not only to isolation and loneliness, but tensions regarding who belongs where also lead to exclusion in both public and private life; while opportunity is often linked to ethnicity (155), once again women are doubly excluded. On the national level, Benazir Bhutto was extremely popular, the Daughter of the East, the first woman Prime Minister of Pakistan, yet because she was a woman was despised by her defeated political opponents as well as the mullahs:

> [The mullahs] were confronted with a catastrophe worse than they could have foreseen. A woman, who under the dictates of Shariat law could not be allowed to lead prayer and whose testimony in court would be counted as only half of a man's, was now taking the oath of office to lead the Islamic Republic of Pakistan (143).

She would, of course, be forced into exile and ultimately killed. The legal caution for such exclusion of women from public life is largely based on General Ziaul Haq's promulgation of laws designed to that effect; Shamsie reminds us that even Benazir Bhutto lost favor with the women's movement because: 'They had been her staunch supporters yet saw her elected into office twice without making any move to repeal the Hudood Ordinances, or even to open discussion on the matter' (61). *The Upstairs Wife* is understandably critical of Zia's legacy, as are many of the works published by the current generation of Pakistani Anglophone writers. Polygamy, Aunt Amina's curse, becomes a national cause as well, in the person of Hamida Bogra, the wife of Prime Minister Mohammad Ali Bogra, when she too becomes the second wife without her consent, leading to a campaign for improved women's rights:

> Mrs. Bogra declared war against Mr. Bogra and all Pakistani men, who now, new arrivals in a Muslim country, believed that they had suddenly been given a license to marry, in accordance with Quranic injunction, one or two or three or even four women. [...] If India threatened their borders, the women agreed, polygamy threatened their marriages. An Islamic Republic could not be allowed to be a Republic of men, men who could secretly wed again and again and yet again (43–4).

Khan notes that 'Mohajir women engaged in organized, collective forms of activism', valorizing their status not only as migrants but as women. Khan gives the example of the MQM, which:

> represents the largest case of women's mobilization since 1947. It is vocal in its pro-women's rights stance, hosts a high-profile women's

organisation with 400 active members in Karachi and 300 in interior Sindh. Sheen recalls a celebrated enlistment in 1989 when, in one day 7,500 women workers swore oaths of allegiance to MQM and were photographed in the papers wearing red, white and green *dupattas* and bangles in the MQM colours (113; Farrukh Sheen 206).

On a more personal level, Aunt Amina suffers from second-class status as well, not only as a woman but as a second wife, which places her in much the same outsider status as a widow, because she is no longer part of a pair, defined by a unique relation to a man. Describing her grandmother, Zakaria recounts how unpaired women enter a zone of exclusion:

> I never saw any woman surface again. [...] Like all the other widows, women who faced the task of justifying a lone existence in a strictly paired world, my grandmother's sudden submersion into seclusion brought on by her husband's death became the first step in a transformation from the living into something less (194).

Much of this exclusion, whether personal or political, is premised on the notion of an enemy within, an enemy who threatens the foundation of society or of family, a violence which, according to Moira Fradinger:

> Targets an internal enemy carved out of a previous community of friends: it transforms the brother, the citizen, the daughter, the ancestor, into an enemy. As such, this enemy signifies a crisis of limits: as the figure of an interior transformed into an exterior, it preserves its interiority at the same time that it becomes foreign [...] The creation and elimination of this enemy figures the temporary fantasy of a binding of the community (4).

Fradinger goes on to say that 'the reification of difference as the other, the impure, the insect, the barbaric, the savage [...] may be a symptom of a failure to articulate the full consequences of our narrative of universal equivalence' (247), thus dehumanizing the other and making his/her elimination that much easier to justify what she calls 'binding violence':

Binding violence represents the desire for, and failure of, a similar closure in terms of the system we identify as an autonomous political community, which we can rephrase as the desire and impossibility to close the gap between the universal abstract ideal of equality (universal political membership) and its concrete determinations (5).

Examples include India, of course, the enemy next door, yet with whom Pakistan has so much in common. It includes East Pakistan, fellow Muslims and fellow Pakistanis, yet by 1971 bitter enemies, as seen from the western wing. And there are the Bihari Muslims, the 'migrants of defeat' (Zakaria 89), herded into Orangi Town, loyal to the project of Pakistan and hence traitors to Bengali independence. And always there are the migrants, the refugees, the immigrants, guilty of what Zygmunt Bauman calls 'the unforgivable sin of late entry', and as such, according to Peter Morey and Amina Yaqin, they disturb 'nativist myths of a timeless national past' (Bauman 59; Yaqin and Morey 37). *The Upstairs Wife* contains many descriptions of refugee massacres and retaliations, including the bombing of Bohri Bazaar on 14 July 1987, which destroyed 'the merchant relic from the city's early days as a magnet for migrants' (Zakaria 101). And as has been said, women especially must be closely supervised lest they disturb the order of things, whether a woman be Prime Minister or a second wife, or an inmate of Karachi's Central Jail, imprisoned on charges of adultery. Most of these women, imprisoned under the Hudood Ordinances, were in fact granted amnesty by Benazir Bhutto, yet would remain the enemy within, forever inside yet ostracized:

> The released women sat on the steps, waiting and wailing. They had nowhere to go, as the families they had left behind did not wish to take them back. In their eyes these women were 'dirty', and no one knew what to do with them. 'Think of your sisters', one mother said over the telephone in the warden's office. 'Who will marry them if you return and remind everyone of your sins?' (146).

It has been suggested that the story of the family is ultimately the story of Pakistan, linking historical account to personal experience, thus creating something more than history. In the case of *The*

Upstairs Wife, this something more includes an array of women's voices which have moved to the foreground, the voices which often go unheard in official historical archives. If the family is a metaphor for the nation, polygamy becomes the image of a double exclusion, first as migrant, second as woman. The immigrant, the 'dirty' woman, the upstairs wife: they have no place to go, and no one seems to know what to do with them. Zakaria asks us to consider whether such a situation is really the way our society should be, or whether it could be otherwise, given that the status quo transforms human beings within our own communities 'from the living into something less' (194).

4

Life-writing and Cultural Memory

Basharat Peer's *Curfewed Night: A Frontline Memoir of Life, Love, and War in Kashmir*

Kashmir, that fabled paradise-on-earth, is regularly in the news, but for the wrong reasons. It is most often mentioned as the point of friction between two nuclear-armed neighbours in South Asia. Apart from some occasional noise by the United Nations and the international community calling for plebiscites, restraint, and bilateral negotiations, the violence in Kashmir makes the headlines from time to time; then, it is largely forgotten by those who don't live there. Basharat Peer was born and raised there, and his memoir of life in Kashmir in the 1980s and 1990s (published in 2010) combines good journalism with personal experience, the kind of life-writing that highlights, not only the details of the everyday, but orients the reader morally and politically. Life-writing is not restricted to the genres of biography, autobiography, or memoir, but can easily include fictional works as well, and as we will see even a memoir does not rely solely on the author's memory but includes other sources, documents, histories, myths and traditions, and so on. As such, the generic boundaries between fiction, memory, and 'fact' are already permeable, and should remain that way in order to encourage what Max Saunders calls 'routes into cultural memory' (322). Saunders goes on to say that cultural memory 'is concerned not with actual events but their cultural repercussions; not with actual memories but with memories as representations […] as representations or mediations or narrativizations of the event, they have always begun to turn the event into something else' (330, 323). That 'something else' means something more than archival history (see Steinmetz 89), more than recollections of past events, more than individual memories, with the goal of writing the self and the collectivity, recording marginalized voices, insisting that things could be otherwise, and as we will see, sometimes therapy for the author and his/her community. Such therapeutic life-writing and production of cultural memory become necessary in any society which is 'far too intimate with violence' (Peer 79). *Curfewed Night* is not simply an individual memoir but that of an entire generation, its specific historical situation and collective cultural memories, and a representation of the past and its repercussions with a view toward the future.

Curfewed Night is a memoir of both lived experience in the 1980s and 1990s and a retrospective/introspective return years later. Although we can and do consider cultural memory in a broad sense across a given community, such sentiments are often at their strongest within one generation, in this case the generation of young men who were physically present at the time, those who grew up amidst the militants and soldiers, many becoming militants themselves. Jürgen Reulecke calls this phenomenon 'generationality', saying 'generation and generationality are, in the end, not tangible entities but rather mental, often very zeitgeist-dependent constructs through which people, as members of a specific age group, are located or locate themselves historically, and accordingly create a we-feeling' (119). In Peer's memoir, such a feeling of historical location is illustrated by a comment such as 'The war of my adolescence had started' (15), or a question that is more than a question:

> Are you a Kashmiri?' a wiry man with dishevelled curly hair and a beaklike nose asked. I smiled back. Both his nose and his question were very Kashmiri. The question asked in Kashmiri was a greeting, a question one Kashmiri asks another Kashmiri in any situation, in any corner of the world, the moment he realizes his companion is

from Kashmir. I have answered and asked this question. It comes with an informal smile and more questions aimed at placing you in Kashmir (97).

Although physical space and linear time are essential elements within a generational context—people who find themselves in the same geographical place at the same time, in this case, Indian-occupied Kashmir of the 1980s and 1990s—it takes more than that to go beyond what Karl Mannheim called 'generational location' to 'generational connection' and ultimately to 'generational consciousness' (Mannheim 528; see also Reulecke 120). Issues of socio-economic class within a given generation should be considered—for example, those who have the financial means to simply leave Kashmir have more options open to them—but more strikingly in *Curfewed Night*, it is the question of gender that comes to the fore. This memoir of war in Kashmir is generally focused on young men, many of whom shared the experience of prison and torture; but there were also young women who composed roughly half of this generation, yet it is safe to say that a memoir written in this context by a woman would undoubtedly 'locate' itself differently. Time too is not the linear time of clocks, but rather the lived time, the *durée* that Henri Bergson and others elucidate; the author himself understands *la durée*: 'I looked at my watch again and turned toward the door. It stood still, wooden. I sat down on the floor and stared at the door. I was somewhat numb. The anticipation of interrogation is worse than the interrogation' (Peer 51–2). Citing Bergson, David Middleton and Steven D. Brown tell us, in this regard, 'life must be characterized by the "uncertainty" found in this small example of being made to wait' (246; see Bergson, *Creative Evolution* 93).

This generation of Kashmiris, these people who grew up during the war, have shared events during their formative years, and further, continue to share the consequences of those events in the form of a collective consciousness, or what Maurice Halbwachs has called 'a spiritual reality' (410; see also Marcel and Mucchielli 141). Even when discussing individual memories as presented in a memoir, the broader social context is essential to the foundation of cultural memory, as Reulecke suggests:

> Studying historical contexts with the generational approach [...] connects the identification of general structures and processes, especially those of various social levels, with the subjective perceptions and experiences of contemporaries, including their interpretations, spheres of action and options for action. [...] With such an approach, the individual is left his unmistakable historicity within the framework of his realm of experience as well as his life story, with a view not least towards his actions in light of the future open to him (121).

As we will see later, life-writing such as *Curfewed Night* is not simply concerned with the past but the present and future as well, already anticipated when Peer tells the reader, 'Time and again I look back and try to cull from memory the moment that was to change everything I had been and would be' (15). In January 1990, protesters took to the streets as a response to Indian aggression, and Peer recalls the moment when he first became part of something bigger, the collective conscience, the aforementioned spiritual reality:

> I felt anger spread in me. [...] Amid the collision of bodies, the holding of hands, the interlocking of eyes in affirmation and confirmation, the merging of a thousand voices, I had ceased to be a shy, bookish boy hunched by the expectations of my family. I wasn't scared of being scolded anymore; I felt a part of something much bigger. I let myself go fly with the crowd. *Aazadi!* (16–18).

This merging of a thousand voices should be taken literally in terms of social or cultural memory; Marcel and Muccielli, referring to Halbwachs' *Les cadres sociaux de la mémoire*, suggest that such collective memorial landmarks become structures of support for other memories, facilitating group membership by:

> locat[ing] memories using social frames built from our present identity [...] for his point is that the past is not really preserved in the individual memory. 'Fragments' persist there, but not complete recollections. What makes them true memories are collective representations (142).

In the memoir, the city of Srinagar becomes such a collective memorial landmark:

> Srinagar is also a greeting, an encounter with a confidant on every street. It is not providing contexts and chronologies to my stories and not explaining the details and the meanings. It is conveying more in a single spoken phrase than in paragraphs and pages in my adopted languages. It is talking endlessly about our shared past, not so much the remote historical past but the recent past—of the fairytale childhood of the eighties and the horror of the nineties (110).

Jeffrey K. Olick too reminds us that, from a Durkheimian perspective, 'culture is not reducible to what is in people's heads' (156), by which he means that cultural memory is resistant to being forgotten or escaped, as dominant institutions play a role in promoting some versions of history more than others, not to mention commemorations and monuments which stimulate public recollection, as well as the important role of myths, folklore, tradition, and such in cultural memory. He concludes, 'There is either a "deep structure" or stored up legacy of shared culture which binds us together; without its pervasive influence, there is no "us" to bind' (156–7). Examples of resistant memories are numerous in *Curfewed Night*: fear becoming routine (46); the school occupied by the military (56); the news being mostly concerned with body counts (104); memorials for the disappeared young in Srinagar (109); seeing Srinagar as a local and knowing its history, 'seeing a bridge, a clearing, a nondescript building and knowing that men fell here, that a boy was tortured there' (115); and never forgetting the 'militants and soldiers. They had shadowed every life I wrote about, including my own. Yet they remained ghostlike presences' (193).

Many of these individual and cultural memories are traumatic, and can result in a cultural aphasia, in other words a disorder in the relations and/or communication between the individual and his/her group (see Marcel and Mucchielli 143; see also Halbwachs 69). Often, those who experience war firsthand have difficulty in speaking about their experience, and it often falls to the next generation to record the stories of those who were there, as Reulecke makes clear: 'Grave changes generally lead, first immediately afterwards and then again at a distance of one to two decades, to society-wide debates about the generational background and results of these events' (120). Peer tells the reader, at several points in *Curfewed Night*, of his difficulties in writing about these events which are too close to be examined objectively, of memory blocking recollection, leaving him unable to communicate. At the beginning of the war, he tells us, 'I fail to remember the beginnings. I fail to remember who told me about *aazadi*' (15). After news of a bomb blast that nearly killed his parents, on the trip home he says, 'I remember nothing else' (70). Trying to recount his experiences of war to friends in Delhi, we learn, 'I could never say everything. I would find myself stopping in the middle of a sentence, rendered inarticulate by memory. The telling, even in the shade of intimacy, was painful' (95). On seeing a boy, covered in a pile of bloody, dead bodies, emerge alive, 'Memories like that disturb me. But I was not the only one; there are hundreds like me' (119), insisting on the collective nature of such memories of war. One example in particular highlight a sort of cultural aphasia, also very difficult to overcome. Many of the men who were tortured have been rendered impotent, and Peer recounts a conversation with one of the victims:

> Hussein seemed to have surrendered to his fate. I struggled to find the right words. Sexuality was almost never discussed in our culture, and impotence was even harder to talk about. I began telling him about Shafi, Ansar, Papa-2, and the medical correction of torture-imposed disorders. He listened in silence, for the most part expressionless. Finally, he began to talk about his experience (140).

When trying to write, Peer explains, 'But I had no distance from the experiences I was trying to process and shape into words' (144), although he will manage to overcome his difficulties, telling a friend, 'I did not forget anything when I was away. I came back to write about Kashmir [...] I had to confront my own ghosts' (144–5), much like the aforementioned victim of torture who was finally able to speak of his experience after encountering a listener from his generation who was able to understand and identify with his situation.

We have been discussing generationality as a building-block of cultural memory, yet it also becomes clear that the generational connection established by one generation—those growing up in Indian-occupied Kashmir in our example—can be passed along to successive generations as well. As we have said, it often becomes the task of the following generation to tell the stories that were blocked by first-generation aphasia, whether individual or collective, as Reulecke explains:

> [A given generation's formative experiences] can, it is true, not be passed on directly, but they do indeed flow, in the form of memory contents created through later selection, attribution, interpretation, etc., into the generative succession as well as into the subjective positioning in one's own 'temporal *Heimat*.' They can also be a legacy intentionally offered to posterity in the form of narratives, bequeathed works, institutions, designed places, and more, and also, according to Freud, engraved in subsequent generations even without an expressed intention to pass them on, although these later generations might also (consciously or unconsciously) reject, re-interpret, or erase them (123).

Peer's memoir falls clearly into the category of 'a legacy intentionally offered to posterity', a realistic record of the human suffering in Indian-occupied Kashmir, an effort to challenge the seeming indifference of those actors who have the power to change the situation. While the first generation can be a motive force for moral and ethical guidance and ultimately political change, as we will see later, it is the durability of cultural memory—and cultural trauma, as part of that memory—over time which can also inform and influence possible futures that are open to a community.

If indeed a generation possesses and projects a certain representation of itself, as we have said, it is through a blending of 'factual' history, memory, and fiction. Generic boundaries are less rigid in what has been called 'faction', or non-fiction novels (which would include, at least to a degree, much Pakistani Anglophone fiction as representative of historical fiction), and I would suggest that such generic permeability works the other way around too, with memoir as a similarly permeable genre. Birgit Neumann and others call such works 'fictions of memory' which both 'depict the workings of memory' and refer to 'the stories that individuals or cultures tell about their past to answer the question 'who am I?', or, collectively:

> who are we?' […] more often than not, they turn out to be an imaginative (re)construction of the past in response to current needs […] consisting of predispositions, biases, and values, which provide agreed-upon codes for understanding the past and present (334).

Curfewed Night is a memoir, and as such a necessarily hybrid creature which, thanks to that flexibility, becomes a representation of cultural memory, a cultural document in its own right, and perhaps an archival document in historical terms which purports to record what 'really' happened (see Saunders 330). In the modernist period and the accompanying rise of scientific methodology, Olick reminds us, record-keeping became more objective and systematic, more like what we have been calling the archive; Henri Bergson regretted the lack of meaningful subjective connection with the past, and proposed memory as the solution to this imbalance, not simply 'passive storage' but:

> active engagement […] Whereas new forms of record keeping measured time and recorded history in increasingly uniform and standardized ways, individual memory was still highly variable, sometimes recording short periods in intense detail and long periods in only the vaguest outline (Olick 154).

Halbwachs then further proposed a distinction between 'autobiographical memory' and 'historical memory,' differentiating between recollection of direct, personal experience and the traces of events left over as a result of cultural memory's durability over time, as a function of group belonging (see Olick 156). This *métissage* of the real and the imaginary is a perfectly normal mechanism in the creation and conservation of cultural memory, and Peer's memoir is no exception, blending memory with archival history as well as myths and traditions, and as a political text certainly participates in 'active engagement.' Early on, we are given the historical context dating to Partition in 1947, and the accession to India signed by Hari Singh, the compromises and evolutions since then, as well as the mention of Yasin Malik, leader of the Jammu and Kashmir Liberation Front (13–14).

These, and many other examples in *Curfewed Night* could rightly be called history in its (more or less) archival, 'factual' definition; real people, dates, events that have been objectively recorded. But Kashmir, the geographical territory across time, is also a cultural and political space permeated by myths, legends, traditions, all part of what we might call the cultural baggage that everyone carries. Among the myths which form the cultural background of *Curfewed Night* are those of Farhad and Shirin, he, cutting through the mountains for his beloved (18) or Hari Parbat, the hill overlooking Srinagar which recalls the creation of Kashmir—when Parvati dropped a pebble to kill an underwater demon, which then became the hill (127). A pre-Islamic past is recalled as well, the Buddhist religion becoming prominent under Emperor Asoka, or the Gandharan style of sculptures from the region, showing Greek traits and testifying to the former presence of Alexander the Great (111–12). At one point, Peer is happy to discover that the legend surrounding Heemal's spring, dedicated to an ancient Kashmiri princess, is alive and well (208). He also recalls a childhood visit to Martand temple, built, according to legend, by the Pandavas, 'the five heroes of *The Mahabharata*,' hence Hindu; before the armed conflict, Hindus and Muslims lived in harmony, and Peer now wonders if the temple would also be occupied by the military (185). These and other myths that we might call fictions are nonetheless important in the creation and maintenance of cultural memory as well as the connection among and between generations.

Intertextuality is important in this cultural mix too; a novel of a young Afghan boy who fought the Russians, *Pahadoon Ka Beta* (19) is mentioned, or the film *Lion of the Desert*, celebrating Libyan resistance to the occupying Italians (20). Nehru, Gandhi, Vàclav Havel, and the Dalai Lama are all mentioned by Peer's father as independence fighters through non-violent means (30), and while all of those heroes were of course genuine historical figures, they have also achieved mythical status around the world, making it sometimes difficult to assess where 'fact' ends and myth begins. Peer pays tribute to revolutionary writers who have gone before, connecting far-off wars to Kashmir and his own memories: Hemingway's *Farewell to Arms*, for example, and Orwell's *Homage to Catalonia*, from which Peer 'developed an obsession with his merging of the personal and the political, the small details and the big ideas' during the 1936 anti-fascist uprising in Barcelona (63), going on to say 'I found [Orwell] giving voice to my attraction to the Kashmiri rebellion as a teenager, which was rooted more in emotional truths than in theories of politics and knowledge of history' (64). This single sentence, 'rooted more in emotional truths …', could well serve as a concise definition of cultural memory. Inspiration is also sought from the successful revolutions in Berlin and Prague, though Kashmir would instead face increased repression; Peer laments the lost opportunity of an alternative possible future: 'if India had allowed those peaceful demonstrations [...] Maybe those demonstrations would have become the dominant force of politics in Kashmir; Indians and Kashmiris could have talked, and thousands of deaths might have been avoided' (132). During the uprisings, hardline Islamists would also confront Kashmiri Muslim practices, with the arrival of Salafist missionaries (167), who condemned 'the way Islam had been practiced over centuries in Kashmir—a mixture of text and tradition' (Ibid.), and Peer tells us that most Kashmiris still resist 'a Saudi-style Islamic code' (171) simply because it does not correspond to their cultural norms. Islam, or indeed any religion, has been used in many times and places for political purposes, yet the violence in Kashmir between the Jamaat-e-Islami and the counterinsurgent forces Ikhwan-ul-Muslimoon, armed by India, was especially brutal (170–1). Peer recounts the continuing influence of Sufi tradition, largely through the history of Nooruddin Rishi, the patron saint of Kashmir: 'He travelled throughout Kashmir, talking to people in their own language. His interpretation of Islam was rooted in the local traditions and culture; the masses understood him better than the Iranian and central Asian Sufis who had brought Islam to Kashmir. He was critical of the orthodox Muslim priests and the Brahmins for reducing religion to empty ritual, turning it into a means of self-promotion, and fueling hatred among the followers of Hinduism and Islam' (181). Summarizing this long history of cultural hybridity, Peer thinks to himself, '*Civilizations leave debris like lovers do*' (114; original italics).

This 'debris' does not simply remain in the past, remembered yet untouched, but impacts the present, and in doing so impacts the future(s) as well. Neumann suggests that:

> [such texts] illuminate the manifold functions that memories fulfill for the constitution of identity. Such texts highlight that our memories are highly selective, and that the rendering of memories potentially tells us more about the rememberer's present, his or her desire and denial, than about the actual past events (333).

Ultimately, the goal is the creation of meaning from multiple sources, what Neumann calls 'productive interpretive possibilities [...] a constructive way to encounter the world', not simple descriptions of the past but, at least to a degree, its producers as well (333-4). Cultural memory is a vast grey zone, consisting of memories, constructions, influences, facts, contradictions and beliefs, a mix of the imaginary and the real, and new perspectives as the process of cultural memory follows its winding, evolving course. As we have said, the creation of meaning is a primary objective, what Neumann calls 'identity-creating constructions of a "usable past"' (338); when discussing *Curfewed Night*, such a usable past resonates politically, as a call for change in the future, as a moral and ethical appeal to insist that things could be other than the way they are. If social change is the goal, the question comes up, what kinds of possible futures are open to us, although the questions might seem a bit wrongheaded, especially if we take seriously Vilém Flusser's remark that we always and everywhere occupy the present. While the discourse of progress would have us believe that time approaches us from the past and heads toward the future, for Flusser it is clear that 'the future advances toward us in our here and now from all directions' (66). In any case, the importance of the present is undeniable, and goes a step further to justify what we have said before, that much of memoir and cultural memory is more concerned with present issues in its retrospection/introspection of past history and experience as it seeks to construct meaning. The question then arises, what kinds of possible futures does one wish to structure from our contemporary present/past? In other words, not simply answering those questions of identity we'd asked earlier, Who am I? Who are we? but also, Where do we want to go from here? Where can we go from here? Or, keeping Flusser in mind, perhaps the question should be, What kinds of present/past do we want to create in order to favor certain outcomes when the future comes our way, to avoid becoming what Peer's poet-teacher called 'the non-beings of the world' (190)? David Middleton and Steven D. Brown suggest that the key to linking past and future is:

> to focus on imaginary futures in the past. Experience […] matter[s] not so much in terms of what happened in the past but in terms of how we build the past with the future in ways that make for the possibility of becoming different. In other words, how we actualize alternative *trajectories of living* (241; original italics).

Much like the example provided by Peer's father in the memoir when speaking of Nehru and Gandhi and Havel: 'None of them used guns, but they changed history. If you want to do something for Kashmir, I would say you should read' (30). Neumann links this concept directly to literary representations:

> Characteristically, fictions of memory are presented by a reminiscing narrator or figure who looks back on his or her past, trying to impose meaning on the surfacing memories from a present point of view. […] Events that took place in the past are recollected only later, i.e., in the present, and are represented as the memories experienced by a narrator or a figure. The constitutive characteristic of all fictions of memory is therefore their operating with co-present time perspectives: The multi-temporal levels of the past and the present intermingle in manifold and complex ways. This kind of organization does not merely establish a consecutive order, not

merely a chain of elements along the arrow of time, but a reference frame in which each event is related to others in both a forward and backward direction: Each event is both marked by all preceding events and evokes expectations about events to come (335–6).

When looked at this way, we are better able to highlight the political aspect of such representations of cultural memory: world-creation, ideas of self and collectivity, sanctioned and unsanctioned memories, pluralities of world views, moral and ethical orientation, all with the goal of communicating this generation's experience to others and instigating social change, what Neumann calls a 'laboratory in which we can experiment with the possibilities for culturally admissible constructions of the past' (see Neumann 335, 341). In our discussion of *Curfewed Night*, a culturally admissible construction of the past would not refer to censorship by this or that institution regarding how history is to be officially represented, but rather a past which anchors cultural memory, including its traumas, in all of its facts, fictions and memories with a focus on its repercussions in the present as the future arrives from all directions.

In a narrative of progress, there would be a teleological 'and they all lived happily ever after' ending to the story, but Peer knows that is not to be when he tells the reader 'The journey was not over; it will never be [...] The conflict might leave the streets, but it will not leave the soul', suggesting that Kashmir and Kashmiris are indeed stuck in a present/past that will not pass (217). Like a traumatic memory that continues to haunt, the Line of Control becomes the concrete symbol of 'That failure of the subconscious [...] And it ran through our grief, our anger, our tears, and our silence' (220–1). Yet, for all of the scars, physical and psychological, Peer's memoir is preparing the ground for a better future, hoping:

> that someday the war they were fighting and the reasons for its existence would disappear like footsteps on winter snow [...] There was no fear that evening. There were only hands reaching out of the bus windows, waving in the air, as if each wave would erase the lines of control (216, 221).

It is an imaginary future perhaps, but possible futures are imagined in the way the past is represented, to our generation and those that follow, in the hope of representing history in such a way that history allows the future to become something else, something more, something better.

5

Neoliberal 'Self-Help' and Water Resources

Mohsin Hamid's *How to Get Filthy Rich in Rising Asia*

Mohsin Hamid's novel, *How to Get Filthy Rich in Rising Asia* (2013), is both a celebration of the 'resilience and potential' of Asia's young generation and a condemnation of neoliberal economic policies which guarantee wealth for a portion of Asia's people while doing little or nothing to eradicate poverty for hundreds of millions of others (Hamid 224). Presented as a self-help book, the novel is a subtle critique of rampant corruption in a rapidly-evolving and resource-stressed Asia, and more precisely for our purposes, South Asia. In contemporary South Asia, self-help is exactly that, the neoliberal individualism which, since Reagan and Thatcher, has gone global in spite of the post-independence socialism envisioned by Nehru. Many analysts credit the market-oriented reforms of 1991 in India, which coincided with the breakup of the Soviet Union, with creating the conditions for South Asia's spectacular economic growth:[1]

> neoliberalism was accompanied by a new set of antipoverty initiatives that stressed self-help and emphasized that the poor could take the initiative and use the market to help themselves rather than rely on government assistance and handouts. The new buzzwords were *empowerment*, *microcredit*, and *entrepreneurialism* (Akhil Gupta 241–2; see Sharma).

However, a more nuanced examination reveals that in spite of a long period of economic boom, abject poverty is still far too common and far too easily accepted. All too often, Asia's wealth has not trickled down, and the neoliberal mantra of a rising tide lifting all boats is exposed as a lie (Gupta 285). Hamid's realist fiction begins with an image of such poverty, and reminds us of the overwhelming odds against escaping its vicious cycle, in spite of Asia's impressive growth; we find the protagonist with his mother in their single mud-walled room:

> [...] huddled, shivering, on the packed earth under your mother's cot one cold, dewy morning. Your anguish is the anguish of a boy whose chocolate has been thrown away, whose remote controls are out of batteries, whose scooter is busted, whose new sneakers have been stolen. This is all the more remarkable since you've never in your life seen any of these things. The whites of your eyes are yellow, a consequence of spiking bilirubin levels in your blood. The virus afflicting you is called hepatitis E. Its typical mode of transmission is fecal-oral. Yum. It kills only about one in fifty, so you're likely to recover (4).

Despite his extremely humble origins, the protagonist will indeed rise out of poverty, but in an environment of omnipresent corruption one must be willing to pay a very high price, take enormous risks, and compromise along the road to wealth. Many of the novel's chapter titles such as 'Avoid Idealists', 'Be Prepared to Use Violence', 'Befriend a Bureaucrat', or 'Patronize the Artists of War' leave no doubt as to the shady ethics involved, all the more so since the 'product' being peddled should, in theory, belong to everyone: Water. Taken for granted until relatively recently, water is becoming increasingly scarce, the new oil, in both economic and political/strategic terms. Water-rights conflicts in South Asia are nothing new, but Hamid's novel brings the debate over poverty, corruption and access to water down to a personal, human scale as a way of exposing the everyday reality of unethical wealth when a basic necessity—a common wealth—is appropriated for the benefit of the few.

Poverty, according to Akhil Gupta, is a form of structural violence in that it is 'taken for granted in the routinized practices of state institutions such that it disappears from view and cannot be thematized as violence at all' (5). He suggests that poverty becomes normal through bio-politics, or the creation of a bureaucratic category of 'poor' through statistical analyses and the definition of a 'poverty line', for example. Such a categorization ultimately results in bureaucratic indifference, which is not necessarily to be taken as a synonym for 'uncaring' but rather the fact that bureaucratic terminologies lead to arbitrary decisions, wherein some of the poor receive aid and some do not (Gupta 42, 58, 158–9). A solution, Gupta goes on to propose, would be to consider poverty-related deaths as preventable, as abnormal, as unacceptable, a form of 'thanatopolitics', which would refuse such official indifference (6). Much of Asia's poverty exists in the villages and countryside, and although improved farming methods and irrigation have contributed to a certain degree of food security, which 'laid the foundation for Asia's rise', the agricultural sector has nevertheless been largely neglected in terms of wealth redistribution (Brahma Chellaney 33).[2] Hamid's novel highlights the 'yawning gap that exists between countryside and city', and makes clear that its protagonist cannot become rich if he remains in the village: 'Moving to the city is the first step to getting filthy rich in rising Asia' (Hamid, *Filthy Rich* 132; 15). Urbanization of the economy, the concentration of goods and services in the big cities and megacities of Asia, means that the poor are very often living right next to the rich, yet are not necessarily less invisible. Such proximity is one of the first things the novel's protagonist notices:

> Your city is not laid out as a single-celled organism, with a wealthy nucleus surrounded by an ooze of slums. It lacks sufficient mass transit to move all of its workers twice daily in the fashion this would require. It also lacks, since the end of colonization generations ago, governance powerful enough to dispossess individuals of their property in sufficient numbers. Accordingly, the poor live near the rich. Wealthy neighbourhoods are often divided by a single boulevard from factories and markets and graveyards, and those in turn may be separated from the homes of the impoverished only by an open sewer, railroad track, or narrow alley. Your own triangle-shaped community, not atypically, is bounded by all three. (Hamid, *Filthy Rich* 20)

The enormous gap between the very rich and the very poor in big cities is put into stark terms in the novel, wherein the young apprentice will 'leap from my-shit-just-sits-there-until-it-rains poverty to which-of-my-toilets-shall-I-use affluence' (78) in an urban environment where 'excessive fertility' is not an asset as it was in the village, and indeed where overpopulation already disturbs the 'balance between population size and available natural resources, including water, food, and energy' (Hamid 38; Chellaney 55). In the novel, the city is presented as a living, if sickly, organism, literally absorbing life from the countryside, whether from the vegetable farmer who has recently become rich by selling his land to local developers or the freeways under construction, 'dusty new arteries feeding this city, which despite its immensity is only one among many such organs quivering in the torso of rising Asia' (82). Chellaney further cautions that rapid Asian urbanization, with a sixty per cent increase in urban population by 2025 predicted by the Asia Society, will continue to stress vital resources, especially water (13; see Asia Society 9).

Once our protagonist has become a city dweller, one of the next self-help steps is to avoid idealists, especially those who might believe in environmental protection, or legal norms, or truth in advertising. Indeed, idealists 'are by their very nature anti-self' (Hamid 57). Hamid's protagonist will associate, albeit briefly, with different sorts of idealists during his truncated time at university, knowing as his father did that getting ahead requires 'advanced schooling and rampant nepotism' (59). University education, however, very quickly disappoints even the most ardent idealist:

> State-subsidized though it may be, your university is exquisitely attuned to money. A small payment and exam invigilators are willing to overlook neighbourly cheating. More and someone else can be sat in your seat to write your paper. More still and no writing is needed, blank exam books becoming, miraculously, a first-class result (60).

The cynical protagonist joins an organization of religious extremists, idealists in their own way, but quickly learns to avoid them as well (60, 73). After an apprenticeship in the distribution of grocery products, in which he learns to undercut competitors' prices by selling expired foods after changing the date of expiration (90), our protagonist then decides to become self-employed—self-help, after all, implies working for oneself—and enter the bottled-water market (99). The product, however, is no less fraudulent, as it is simply tap water packaged in used mineral-water bottles recuperated from restaurants, and the tap water is contaminated as well:

> Your city's neglected pipes are cracking, the contents of underground water mains and sewers mingling, with the result that taps in locales rich and poor alike disgorge liquids that, while for the most part clear and often odourless, reliably contain trace levels of faeces and microorganisms capable of causing diarrhoea, hepatitis, dysentery, and typhoid (Hamid 99).

The protagonist takes care to boil the water (101), knowing that customers falling sick will be bad for business, but also because he understands that great care must be used when presenting a counterfeit product and takes seriously Wambui Mwangi's assertion that 'Forgeries, confusingly, are real until they are not' (115). He goes so far as to install tamper-resistant caps and plastic safety wrapping, for example (100). The poor cannot afford bottled water, and are obliged to drink contaminated tap water, often becoming very ill as a result, while those better off can and do pay the protagonist for his marginally-safer product (marginally safer because boiling does nothing to remove other toxins, such as heavy metals and pesticides). Access to safe drinking water affects the poor more than the rich, although water scarcity will become more and more acute in the near future, affecting everyone, not only in terms of drinking water but water for agriculture, the 'virtual water' which we consume every day without thinking about it. Increasing water consumption, whether real or virtual, does not fit neatly into a rich-vs-poor binary; we must keep in mind that in contemporary Asia, the burgeoning middle class is largely responsible for changing, environmentally-unfriendly habits: equipping their homes with washing machines and dishwashers, and eating much more meat (Chellaney 3). In terms of idealism, the middle class is not politically innocent either, as Gupta insists: 'In a country like India, the perpetrators of violence include not only the elites but also the fast-growing middle class, whose increasing number and greater consumer power are being celebrated by an aggressive global capitalism' (22).[3] The protagonist has consciously chosen to sell a product which is both essential and becoming more and more scarce, illustrating that he has internalized his own advice to avoid idealists: 'You have thrived to the sound of the city's great whooshing thirst, unsated and growing, water incessantly being pulled out of the ground and pushed into pipes and containers. Bottled hydration has proved lucrative' (121). Throughout South Asia, water is becoming increasingly scarce, and available sources increasingly polluted.

Water has become a security issue; whoever controls the water supply has a strategic advantage, whether on an international scale or more modestly, on the scale of a city in South Asia, as in Hamid's novel. No matter what the scale, it is oftentimes difficult to know who is in control; sometimes, many different people and agencies are, whether officially or unofficially. Chapters entitled 'Befriend a Bureaucrat', 'Patronize the Artists of War', and 'Dance with Debt' suggest that the State must be dealt with on many different levels, whether administrative, military, or financial. Our protagonist knows that rather than avoiding the State, it must be offered a partnership if he is to succeed: 'Two related categories of actor have long understood this. Bureaucrats, who wear state uniforms while secretly backing their private interests. And bankers, who wear private uniforms while secretly being backed by the state. You will need the help of both' (Hamid 140). If negotiations with the State bureaucracy are essential in any country, they are particularly complex in South Asia, especially when one is selling a fraudulent product which, by rights, should be provided to everyone. In such a case, Gupta's question, 'Which State?', makes sense:

> When analysts refer to the state, do they mean the state at the federal or central level, at the regional level, or at the local level? Which branch of the state are they studying: the administrative, legislative, or judicial? Which particular bureau are they focusing on: the police,

the revenue department, the education department, the bureau of worker safety, the electricity department, and so forth? [...] Finally, what policies, programmes, and people do they see as constituting the state? (52)

While understanding how the State machinery works is helpful if one wants to get ahead, its complexity is multiplied due to rampant corruption, which requires a certain additional 'cultural capital' to negotiate, as well as the fact that many bureaucrats in rising Asia tend to collapse the boundary between their public and private roles, often operating out of their homes or tea stalls rather than an office in a public building (Gupta 76, 86, 90). Our protagonist has learned over the years and has paid many bribes to remain in business: 'Permits denied, inspections failed, surmounted by greasing junior and mid-level palms' (141). But now that business is even better and our protagonist is seeking a municipal contract, the stakes have been raised and the State must be approached on a higher level. Bribes have been paid to have an appointment with the politician, and the meeting with him is described as something akin to 'the courts of princes of old', the negotiation taking place almost as an aside to other business, including a lunch which the protagonist is not offered, and finally: 'A number is thrown out. This is accepted by you with obsequious murmurs and bows of the head, precisely as you have been instructed to do by the bureaucrat. And that is that' (145). While such a transaction may seem reprehensible, Gupta argues that there is always a degree of corruption in politics, and that such an interaction between a subaltern and a representative of the State is in fact what constitutes a State.[4]

Violence, as we have seen, is often structural—taken for granted, routine, institutional—and the protagonist understands this in profound, even Marxist, terms:

> Distasteful though it may be, it was inevitable, in a self-help book such as this, that we would eventually find ourselves broaching the topic of violence. [...] For wealth comes from capital, and capital comes from labour, and labour comes from equilibrium, from calories-in chasing-calories out, an inherent, in-built leanness, the

leanness of biological machines that must be bent to your will with some force … (119).

Yet our protagonist is also exposed to punctual, direct, physical violence as a result of his desire to dominate the water market, against a backdrop of ongoing social unrest and violence, riots and bombings, in unplanned and overpopulated cities where millions of migrants come to seek a better life (Hamid 119–21). A well-connected local businessman who is losing bottled-water customers hires a thug to threaten the protagonist at gunpoint. Rather than go to the police, he seeks the help of a local armed faction, which furnishes him with a bodyguard; the guard will later kill the thug during a second encounter, thus frightening the local businessman to end his ultimatum (Hamid 123–35). The protagonist's business will continue to prosper yet his brush with death has shattered his belief that wealth would shelter him from a premature death, wherein the victims are almost always the poor. Observing his small son, for example, the protagonist thinks: 'For while disease or violence could of course strike down your son, the probability of his early death has, through your attainments, been reduced dramatically' (146). So, too, on a larger scale, where international tensions and institutional saber-rattling between water-haves and water-have-nots will certainly escalate to armed conflict in the relatively near future, and the wealthy will not be spared:

> Asia, with the world's fastest-growing economies, fastest-rising military expenditures, most dangerous hot spots, and fiercest resource competitions, seems to be the biggest potential flashpoint for water wars in the world—a concern underscored by the attempts of some countries to exploit their riparian advantage (Chellaney 15).

Chellaney goes on to highlight the fact that among the aforementioned hot spots are many countries which share the common obstacles of water scarcity and dysfunctional government, including Pakistan and Afghanistan, and he cites the example of the Israeli Six-Day War in 1967 as, fundamentally, a war over access to the waters of the Jordan River (56, 58). In other words, water is evolving from its role in non-traditional security discussions to a central strategic factor in the traditional security debate, wherein countries are willing to engage in armed conflict over water, much as they have done over oil in the past. Hydropolitics will, Chellaney insists, turn ugly and become violent, especially if spectacular Asian economic growth begins to slow (which it will at some point) due to competition for increasingly scarce resources (90).

When a problem becomes overwhelming, Hamid's self-help book suggests having an exit strategy ready, but one shouldn't wait too long: 'For there was a moment when anything was possible. And there will be a moment when nothing is possible. But in between we can create' (219–20). If we extrapolate that advice to an Asian scale and apply it to the issue of poverty/corruption/access to water, it is clear that the moment when nothing is possible is rapidly approaching, especially when it comes to water. The obvious response is that more international cooperation, and less self-help, is necessary; poverty, for example, is a global problem, yet one of the reasons that global poverty does not go away is that local governments are always tasked with finding solutions (Gupta 239). Strong institutions with a focus on long-range, holistic/biosphere planning with clearly defined norms and objectives are necessary if Asia—and especially South Asia—is to avoid serious future conflict:

> In an era of growing constraints on augmenting the supply of the most essential resource—water—Asian countries must seek sustainable, cost-effective solutions through collaborative efforts that extend beyond national borders. Competing demands for scarce water resources pose economic, social, and political threats that can be contained only through forward-looking policies. Such policies, as well as the promotion of greater interstate and intrastate water collaboration, depend on linking stakeholders together, collecting reliable data on water resources, and enunciating specific, measurable, attainable, realistic, and timely—SMART—goals (Chellaney 305).

Hamid's novel sounds a warning regarding the gap between rich and poor: 'What you do sense, what is unmistakable, is a rising tide of frustration and anger and violence [...] At times, watching the stares that follow a luxury SUV as it muscles its way down a narrow road, you are nearly relieved to have been already separated from your fortune' (205-206). Hamid's protagonist has experienced in microcosm the serious questions which arise when a basic necessity—water—is appropriated by a few rather than shared out fairly; those same questions remain pertinent on a global scale, and misappropriation of our common wealth will inevitably lead to serious conflict and catastrophic consequences in the very near future, and Asia's rise will come to a screeching halt.

Notes

1. The disintegration of the former Soviet Union forced India to overhaul its economic philosophy, as Brahma Chellaney explains: India's rise as a new economic giant was tied to the post-1989 events. India was so much into barter trade with the Soviet Union and its Communist allies in Eastern Europe that when the Eastern Bloc began to unravel, India had to start paying for imports in hard cash. This rapidly depleted its modest foreign-exchange reserves, triggering a severe balance-of-payments crisis in 1991. This financial crisis, in turn, compelled India to embark on radical economic reforms, which laid the foundation for its economic rise.' 19–20.

2. Akhil Gupta cites disagreements between Indian farmers regarding the role of liberalization and globalization as the principal reason for missing the opportunity of economic reforms: 'Unlike the federations of Indian industry (FICCI and FII), which, despite differences among their members, quickly resolved to support liberalization and then used government policy to favor industry as a sector, the peasant movements were hopelessly divided and failed to come up with a unified set of demands for the agricultural sector. The result has been that agriculture has recorded the slowest growth rates of the sectors in the Indian economy. Agriculture is the only place where the vast majority of the unemployed and underemployed population can find employment in the short and medium term, but that will not happen if there is slow growth in this sector (Eswaran, Kotwal, Ramaswami, and Wadhwa 2009). Without significantly increasing growth rates in agriculture, there is little chance that the poor will see a growth in their employment prospects or wages' (284-285). Gupta goes on to qualify his statement, saying that growth in the agricultural sector is nevertheless possible without a corresponding growth in employment if expensive new technologies are employed in farming, a situation which he considers unlikely in India in the near future (326).

3. In an endnote of his own, Akhil Gupta presents John Gledhill's position that global capitalist policies are indeed violent: 'Gledhill (1999) argues that the demands imposed on Third World states by global capitalist enterprises, along with the geopolitical agendas of northern states, sometimes results in the creation of states that kill their own citizens' (Gupta 299).

4. Along these same lines of the subaltern confronting the State is the question of literacy among the poor. While most would argue that literacy is essential as a tool to negotiate with the State on its own terms (where complaints and lawsuits, for example, must be in writing to be taken seriously, and where forms and files are extremely important), Gupta rightly reminds us that a literate population, while perhaps more difficult to exploit, is also more easily formatted to the State's ideology (215; 217). Gupta also suggests that literacy may well be overrated in the history of mankind, given Lévi-Strauss's assertion that writing came after the great Neolithic discoveries: 'the development of agriculture, the domestication of animals, pottery making, and weaving' (Gupta 192-193; see also Lévi-Strauss 1969: 27-28, and 1967: 291). In the novel, the protagonist as a child is the only one of the family who can read the credits after a television film, the TV being 'a sign of [the family's] urban prosperity:' 'When the show is done, credits roll. Your mother sees a meaningless stream of hieroglyphs. Your father and sister make out an occasional number, your brother that and the occasional word. For you alone does this part of the programming make sense. You understand it reveals who is responsible for what' (Hamid 33; italics added).

PART 3 | WAR

6

Pakistan during the Afghan War

History, Legacy, and Contemporary Literary Representations

Although Pakistan, as an independent nation, has only existed as such for about one human lifetime, seventy-five years, the Indus Valley region that would become Pakistan has a centuries-long tradition of cultivating a tolerant, open interpretation of Islam, historically infused with Sufi traditions. Recent decades have, however, seen the rise of conservative Wahhabi Sunni Islam in Pakistan. This has been exported from Saudi Arabia with much success, owing to many factors but especially the 1970s oil shocks, the 1979 Iranian revolution, and the Soviet invasion of Afghanistan in the same year. While Pakistan is currently experiencing many difficulties on many different fronts, hardline Islamists is one of the most serious of its challenges, resulting in sectarian violence as well as contributing to institutional immobility and stagnation in education, culture, and politics, not to mention the situation of women. Although Wahhabi influence has been present on the Indian subcontinent since the eighteenth century, our focus will be contemporary and stress the accelerating fundamentalism in Pakistan since the 1970s. This chapter hopes to give a brief history of the Wahhabi religious tradition in Saudi Arabia, compared to a very different tradition in Pakistan, then examine the Saudi hegemonic project at a precise point in time, beginning in 1977 when Ziaul Haq took control of Pakistan by force of arms with a mission to 'Islamize' society. Then we will consider the legacy, after Zia's death, of this religious imperialism and the current debates, consequences and problems it engenders and how it is represented in the press and in contemporary historical fiction.

The Soviet Union invaded Afghanistan in December 1979, in support of the Afghan communist government, itself having come to power by overthrowing a centrist government in April 1978. Many of the Afghan resistance fighters would seek refuge in Pakistan, thus bringing Pakistan into the war as providing strategic depth and safe haven for the Muslim mujahideen against the invaders, all with the support of Saudi Arabia and the United States. Weapons destined for Pakistan were sent through Saudi Arabia, with CIA support, and Thomas Hegghammer also notes that the Saudi ambassador gave Osama bin Laden logistical support in 1985, moving a bulldozer from Saudi Arabia to Pakistan and then on to a training camp in Afghanistan (27). Although somewhat overlooked, Iran too played a role, not only fearing an extremist Sunni government on its border but also in the continuity of its struggle with Saudi Arabia for regional influence: 'while the US, Saudi Arabia, and Pakistan tended to back mainly Sunni-fundamentalist Pashtun mujahideen groups, like Gulbuddin Hekmatyar's Hezb-e Islami, Iran generally supported Persian-speaking or Shia groups, mainly among the Hazaras. This active Pakistani cooperation with Saudi Arabia and the United States is understandable, given the war in Afghanistan, yet is only the tip of the iceberg regarding Saudi influence in Pakistan. The war, in fact, was a convenient excuse and an opportunity for Pakistani leaders to receive billions of dollars of Saudi and US aid, thus providing the necessary resources for one man, General Ziaul Haq, to pursue a programme of radical Brotherhood/Wahhabi Islamization of Pakistan, which he could not have accomplished otherwise. Pakistan was of course founded in 1947 as a homeland for India's Muslims, and its founding father, Mohammad Ali Jinnah insisted on religious tolerance within the new state, dominated as it was by a Muslim majority, at least if one considers his oft-cited 'secularist' speech to the Constituent Assembly: 'You are free; you are free to go to your temples, you are free to go to your mosques or to any other place of worship in this State of Pakistan. You may belong to any religion or caste or creed—that has nothing to do with the business of the State' (Muhammad Ali Jinnah's first Presidential Address to the Constituent Assembly of Pakistan, August 11, 1947). Jinnah's untimely death left Pakistan without its charismatic founder and opened a breach for his successors, both military and civilian, and often clearly secularist, to exploit Islam for political purposes. The 'modernist' Ayub Khan, for example, had to include 'Islamic' in the official name of the Republic of Pakistan, and Z. A. Bhutto, not known for his religious devotion, excluded the Ahmadi sect in a cold (and often erroneous) political calculation (Marc Gaborieau 246-247). But it was Zia who, well beyond simple political maneuvering, embarked on a mission to Islamize Pakistan along Wahhabi lines.

As we have said, Pakistan—or the territory that would become Pakistan—had for centuries been a Muslim land that had enjoyed relative tolerance of other faiths and between sects, and benefitted from the influence of a more mystical, popular form of Islam, Sufism, including its reverence of saints (Aminah Mohammad-Arif 231). Ayesha Jalal suggests that Pakistan's reputation as a 'relatively liberal and modern Muslim state' continued until the early 1970s, when the Pakistani civil war of 1971 and the loss of the eastern wing created the conditions, even before Zia's accession to power, for an anti-secular backlash and Saudi incursion:

> Unaccustomed to learning from history and more comfortable with myths of an imagined past, Pakistanis were susceptible to the Islamist charge that the ruling elite's lack of religiosity had caused the country's disintegration. […] Lines of credit were sought from friendly Arab states, softening the blows of the global oil shock for cash-starved Pakistan. The global reassertion of Islam on the back of Arab petro-dollars won the admiration of Pakistan's rising middle classes, who sought to emulate the Saudi variant of Wahabi Islam (14-15).

Zulfikar Ali Bhutto became, in spite of concessions to the religious parties, the symbol of Pakistan's decadence, and would be deposed in a coup d'état, then executed, by Ziaul Haq. The transition from one pseudo-Islamic order to another is summarized by Kamila Shamsie:

Prior to Zia, Pakistan's leaders had often raised the banner of Islam as a politically expedient tool, but, apart from Bhutto's banning of the Ahmadis for reasons both political and personal, they had always ensured that Islam remained at best a cosmetic gloss to the functioning of the state. With Zia, that old order was to be turned firmly on its head. [...] Zia's Islam became Pakistan's Islam (*Offence* 46-48).

Unlike Bhutto, Zia was personally very religious and had made several trips to Mecca, and after his seizure of power he was received by the Saudis as a head of state; formal contact with Saudi Arabia was initiated almost immediately after the coup d'état by then-Chief Martial Law Administrator General Mohammed Ziaul Haq (Mehrunnisa Ali, 'Ziaul Haq's Visit to Muslim Countries' 103). In a chapter entitled 'The Diversity of Islam,' Aminah Mohammad-Arif insists that Zia's Saudi-inspired Islamization (and more precisely, Zia's proximity to the Jamaat-i-Islami party founded by Maududi) resulted in the blatant promotion of Sunni Wahhabi Islam and the demonization of the Shia minority; what had been largely doctrinal disputes between the two sects now became more overtly violent (233). Zia's first confrontation with the Shia was related to the payment of alms, or zakat. Zia's attempt to compel the Shia to pay such alms by way of a governmental tax on assets was met with violent resistance which, according to Mohammad-Arif, not only undermined Zia's authority and angered the military, but increased worries that the Iranian revolution was directly politicizing Shia activity in Pakistan (233). Reacting to this fear of the Iranian 'contagion' spreading to Pakistan, Zia embarked on a project to strengthen Sunni educational institutions, notably through the creation of madrasahs, or Koranic schools linked to the major Sunni schools of thought and often funded by Saudi Arabia; the exponential multiplication of madrasahs is one of the major element of Zia's Islamization policies, the effects of which are still being felt today (Mohammad-Arif 233-234). Zia also pushed for extremist reforms in the judicial and political arenas, many of which still remain on the statute books, as Shamsie reminds us:

Lashing, amputation, stoning to death—all in public. Most offensive of all to Muslims for whom theirs was a religion of justice, the Hudood Ordinances allowed for rape victims to be tried for adultery and stoned to death. [...] In 1983, the Islamic Law of Evidence decreed that in legal matters the evidence of two women is equal to that of one man. [...] This was also the year that, under the Hudood Ordinances, Safia Bibi, a blind 13-year-old girl who was raped but couldn't identify her attackers, was found guilty of adultery and sentenced to imprisonment, a fine and a public lashing (Offence 48-49).

The religious parties, especially the JI, couldn't believe their good fortune. After thirty years on the margin, they now had access to power at the highest level; Qadeer reports that in 1978, fully two-thirds of Zia's ministers were appointed from the ranks of the religious parties (166). For the first time since Partition, instead of a secular government which deployed Islam as a political tool, the roles were now reversed: 'Islamists had their opportunity to utilize the state's authority to push their social and cultural agenda. [...] the drive for an Islamic order came to mean changing culture and reorganizing society' (Qadeer 166-167).

The Soviet invasion of Afghanistan and the resulting decade-long war would reinforce the role of the madrassahs as the first step in the process of recruiting and training fighters for the *jihad*, the Holy War, as would Zia's open door policy to international networks of what Olivier Roy calls 'Islamic brigades,' many of which were associated with the Muslim Brotherhood, a policy encouraged and funded by both the United States and Saudi Arabia (140), a policy which would have disastrous effects long after the Soviet withdrawal in 1988:

> [The Afghan jihadis] were heavily subsidized by the Gulf States, especially Saudi Arabia. This Saudi largesse also took the form of training grants, gradually introducing a much more 'Wahhabi' influence which was quite hostile towards local religious traditions, both learned and popular. This was the setting for the development of the movement which became known as the Taliban (140).

The militarization of Islam and the US and Saudi support of international Islamic brigades has created unintended and far-reaching consequences around the globe as these holy warriors have remobilized in other regions after the defeat of the Soviet Union. The paradox is striking; Muslim warriors whose mission was to defeat godless communist invaders are still active in Afghanistan and Pakistan and elsewhere, yet most of their victims are in fact other Muslims, often victims of the ongoing tensions between the Sunni and Shia sects. Saudi Arabia's hegemonic project in Pakistan continues unabated, fanning the flames of sectarian violence with petrodollars; Zia's legacy, rather than uniting Pakistan under the banner of Wahhabi Islam, is instead one of almost daily killing between Muslims themselves, widely reported in the Pakistani press and an important element of contemporary Pakistani historical fiction.

A 2012 article from *Press TV*, entitled 'Carnage of Shia Muslims in Pakistan,' deplores the current situation, qualified as nearly genocidal, before tracing the historical roots of the conflict: 'With thousands of Shia Muslims killed over the past few years in Pakistan and over 400 murdered in recent months, the killings have practically amounted to genocide.' Longstanding institutional complicity regarding anti-Shia violence is taken to be self-evident:

> That the Shia mass murders have continued over the years with no legal and judiciary source or law enforcement agencies having sought to put an end to these brutalities indicates that these acts are but to be considered as part of a systematic and organized plot prodigiously funded and ingeniously engineered by internal and external forces (Ismail Salami).

Salami then goes further back in time, and pinpoints Ziaul Haq as the man 'who made it a state policy to fund and arm Wahhabi groups in the 1980s. It was during those years when he technically institutionalized violence by unleashing the Sipah-Sahaba fundamentalists on Shia-populated regions, ushering in a new age of violence and mayhem'. The most significant episode of this institutionalized violence, the Gilgit massacre of May 1988, is then detailed by Salami, who reminds us that Pakistani intelligence agencies were also monitoring Shia activities in the aftermath of the Iranian revolution. The leaks of diplomatic cables have only confirmed what journalists and historians have long been saying. Pervez Hoodbhoy's 2009 article, 'Is Pakistan Emulating Saudi Arabia?' gives an overview of Zia's legacy of Islamization and arrives at a very pessimistic conclusion:

> For three decades, deep tectonic forces have been silently tearing Pakistan away from the Indian subcontinent and driving it towards the Arabian Peninsula. This continental drift is not physical but cultural, driven by a belief that Pakistan must exchange its South Asian identity for an Arab-Muslim one. Grain by grain, the desert sands of Saudi Arabia are replacing the rich soil that had nurtured a magnificent Muslim culture in India for a thousand years. [...] Now a stern, unyielding version of Islam (Wahhabism) is replacing the kinder, gentler Islam of the Sufis and saints who had walked on this land for hundreds of years.

Hoodbhoy blames Zia in the first instance, citing the Afghan war and other factors that we have already mentioned, and goes on to accuse every succeeding government of cowardice regarding their refusal to significantly overhaul the Pakistani education system, especially its madrassahs, which supplied 'cannon fodder' during the war and today turn out unemployed students who reproduce 'a grim and humorless Saudi-inspired revivalist movement that frowns on any and every expression of joy and pleasure.' Hoodbhoy especially deplores the degraded condition of women, including women from the upper classes who had, for a time, been spared the constraints of their poorer sisters; speaking of his own experience as a university professor, Hoodbhoy laments: 'The Saudi-ization of a once-vibrant Pakistani culture continues at a relentless pace. [...] Many of my veiled female students have largely become silent note-takers, are increasingly timid and seem less inclined to ask questions or take part in discussions.'

Despite other constraints, Pakistan is fortunate in having a functioning free press, which does not shy away from controversial issues, as some of the preceding examples show, both from within and without Pakistan. The Saudi hegemony has also been treated in other forms of nonfiction works, such as essays, theses and the like, and indeed some of Pakistan's most notable fiction writers also write for the press and in other nonfiction media. Kamila Shamsie's *Offence: The Muslim Case* is a prime example. *Offence* charts the rise of Muslim extremism and, while Shamsie is of course extremely critical of Zia and his legacy, she reminds us that it was in fact Z. A. Bhutto who opened the door to Saudi influence and thus made Zia's Islamization programme that much easier:

> 'Bhutto was seeking to extend his influence as a regional leader. In the wake of the 1973 oil crisis, he recognized the oil-producing Arab nations as major power players with whom he wanted to ally himself; his hosting of the Second Islamic Summit was the most visible sign of this. But this new regional association meant allying himself with Saudi Arabia and its ultra-hardline, puritanical Wahabi version of Islam, closely tied to Maududi's JI (42-43).

As we have already mentioned, the Afghan war brought billions of dollars of US and Saudi aid to Pakistan, giving Zia the necessary means to implement his extremist interpretation of Islam, and leaving an unwanted legacy, unwanted at least by the majority of Pakistani Muslims: 'A new generation of Pakistanis was growing up in a world in which the tentacles of Zia's Islam were everywhere' (Shamsie 55). Mohsin Hamid too, in a chapter entitled 'Why Pakistan will Survive,' discusses the question of Pakistani identity from many different perspectives, one being how an average Pakistani might relate to Zia's legacy:

> Similarly, if the test of being a Pakistani is that I would like our country to look more like what Ziaul Haq had in mind—in other words, a country where you could happily live your life according to any interpretation of Islam so long as it was his interpretation of Islam—then I fail again. I don't want my government imposing its view of religion on me. [...] So, I support the idea that Pakistan should be a place where Muslims are free to practice their religion according to their own conscience, and where religious minorities are free to do the same (38-39).

Zia's Islamization policy and its catastrophic consequences on the Muslims of the Indus Valley has made its way significantly into contemporary fictional representations as well; many of the current generation of Pakistani writers whose work can easily be qualified as historical fiction have incorporated Zia's legacy into their accounts. They are, after all, the generation that was born in Zia's shadow. While the most direct, albeit brief, reference to the Saudi connection is found in H. M. Naqvi's *Home Boy*, wherein one of the characters laments the cloud of suspicion that hovers over Pakistanis in the wake of September 11th, reminding the reader that the attackers were, in fact, 'a bunch of crazy Saudi bastards' (146), a more extended treatment of US and Saudi support for Zia is Mohammed Hanif's *A Case of Exploding Mangoes*. Hanif's novel is a fictionalized account of Zia's final days as Pakistan's president and finally his death in a mysterious plane crash, and presents Zia as a religious zealot bent on imposing his Saudi-inspired interpretation of Islam on the entire country. During his first meeting with his Generals after the coup d'état, Zia berates his audience for their lack of religious conviction—not to mention their inability to understand Arabic—and makes it clear that conservative Islam will no longer simply function as a political tool but as official State policy:

> 'The generals who had called Zia a mullah behind his back felt ashamed at having underestimated him; not only was he a mullah, he was a mullah whose understanding of religion didn't go beyond parroting what he had heard from the next mullah. A mullah without a beard, a mullah in a four-star general's uniform, a mullah with the instincts of a corrupt tax inspector [...] In the name of God, God was exiled from the land and replaced by the one and only Allah who, General Zia convinced himself, spoke only through him (33-34).

Zia's direct link with Saudi Arabia is further made explicit in the novel, for example when Zia thinks to himself: 'He wouldn't mind being remembered as Caliph Omar the Second' (221), or in the scene recounting Zia's visit to Mecca, a visit which overwhelms Zia but when seen from the perspective of his security chief becomes a parody:

There were no flashes of divine light, no thunder, the walls of the room were black and without a single inscription. And if it hadn't been for General Zia's choked voice seeking forgiveness, it would have been a quiet room full of stale air. Allah's house was a dark, empty room (157).

US involvement is highlighted as well, with appearances by Ambassador Arnold Raphael, US Secretary of State George Schultz, and CIA Operations Director Bill Casey, not to mention Osama bin Laden's arrival as a guest at the Embassy barbecue (207). Other contemporary Pakistani novels, while not explicitly mentioning a Saudi connection, nevertheless make the Zia legacy an important background for the setting; we could mention Kamila Shamsie's *In the City by the Sea,* wherein a decidedly Zia-like military dictator has imprisoned his main political rival and cast a pall over the once-vibrant city, while plots to depose him are hatched; or Nadeem Aslam's *The Wasted Vigil,* set during the Afghan war during the Zia era, underscoring the damage done, not only by the Soviet invaders, but by the hardliners of Islam as well, never forgetting that the United States' hands were not clean either.

Zia's legacy, and by extension the Saudi-supported Islamization of Pakistan of the late 1970s and 1980s, has left deep scars on Pakistan and, as we have seen, historians, journalists, and novelists have not shied away from condemning Zia as an agent of Saudi influence in the political and cultural fabric of Pakistan. Although Zia was killed in 1988, Saudi incursion into Pakistan's affairs continues unabated, often in the form of Sunni versus Shia violence. We have already mentioned an article entitled 'Carnage of Shia Muslims in Pakistan' from *Press TV,* deploring not only the murders but the lack of institutional response; Kamila Shamsie makes a similar point in a 2013 article in *The Guardian,* entitled 'In Pakistan, there's no Answer to Terror: Pakistan's Government and Military alike are Silent on who is Promoting the Murder of Shias in Baluchistan'. Shamsie says, 'It's symbolic really—Shias are murdered and no one who wants to protest can get anywhere near the president, whose silence can be heard well past the roadblocks.' A 2013 article in *Dawn,* 'Smokers' Corner: Petro Games,' denounces the terrorist attacks against the

Hazara Shia community in Quetta, and the general refusal to ask difficult questions: 'These questions contain nothing new. It's just that most media personnel and politicians in Pakistan have found it hard to ask them. Mainly because they involve an awkward inquiry into the role of some rich, oil producing Arab monarchies in propping up and funding militant Sunni outfits and terror groups in Pakistan' (Nadeem F. Paracha). There are rumors that Saudi Arabia has funded Pakistan's nuclear weapons programme, albeit vigorously denied by Pakistan's Foreign Office (see http://www.dawn.com/news/1054796/pakistan-denies-reports-saudis-funded-nuclear-program). Frédéric Bobin, writing for *Le Monde* from Karachi just before the elections in May 2013, calls the Sunni-Shia rivalry one of the future Prime Minister's biggest challenges; he goes further, citing the opposition's assertion that Nawaz Sharif's Muslim League has in fact supported anti-Shia activities. In an interview with Allama Abbas Kumaili, director of the Jaffaria Alliance [Shia], Bobin quotes him as saying 'An anti-Shia genocide is happening in Pakistan', although ultimately Saudi Arabia is to blame: 'The Saudis have financed these extremist groups [Lashkar-e-Jhangvi] with the goal of imposing a Wahhabi State in Pakistan' (4; my translation). From time to time, there is a glimmer of hope, however; an October 2013 article in *Dawn*, 'A Sensible Call: Haj Sermon,' congratulates the Saudi Grand Mufti regarding his Haj sermon, 'in which the senior cleric called for shunning sectarianism and condemned terrorism, which was much-needed and timely. The symbolic importance of the event cannot be overlooked, as the religious leader spoke to around 1.5 million believers present at Mount Arafat for the largest gathering of Muslims on earth'. Contemporary Saudi influence in Pakistan has functioned on such a grand scale largely due to Saudi foreign aid at a time when Pakistan is dependent on such aid, yet such funding always comes with strings attached; the solution is to cut the strings. Pakistan must concentrate on strengthening its institutions—poor primary education, for example, is a demographic time bomb waiting to explode—and do everything necessary to end economic dependence on the US, Saudi Arabia, and more recently on China: economic development, education leading to employment, a fair and functional tax code. Only then will Pakistan be able to go its own way, and, while not all Pakistanis agree what that way should be, their destiny is certainly one of a South Asian cultural heritage rather than Saudi Arabian, as Asad Badruddin suggests:

> While religion comes from the same source, it is up to different countries and peoples on how to interpret it to enrich their lives. That is why the Islam practiced in Saudi Arabia is different from the one practiced in most of Pakistan. The role of religion (in all of its cultural, spiritual, non-denominational and ritual manifestations) will remain in society. What is important is for thinkers to channel it into a force that is creative and not destructive, inclusive and pluralistic, not one that imposes its will on the unwilling.

Most Pakistanis know this, of course, and many are working to make it happen. Pakistan is home to dynamic universities, a free press and a vibrant literary milieu; these are some of the forums which are necessary to resist Zia's legacy and Saudi and American influence, to denounce sectarian violence, and ultimately to reclaim Pakistan's South Asian Islamic heritage.

7

Cultural Understanding as Military Strategy

Mapping the Human Terrain in Nadeem Aslam's *The Wasted Vigil*

Military strategists have been interested in geographical terrain for millennia: mountains and deserts that must be crossed, rivers that must be bridged, frozen Siberian plains that must simply be survived. The physical features of the landscape must be taken into account and battle plans adapted to the terrain, otherwise failure is assured. The history of contemporary warfare is full of examples of such failures, when cookie-cutter models of combat between two industrial powers are generically applied to situations of irregular conflict. Much more recently, army commanders have recognized the utility of understanding the human terrain / local culture as an important element in long-term strategy, not only as a way to gain the trust of the target population and reduce violent encounters, but also to better ensure victory should fighting recur. With such a goal in mind, the US Army has established Human Terrain Teams which accompany military units in Afghanistan and Iraq. These teams are composed of sociologists, anthropologists, linguists, and other civilian social scientists, for the purpose of 'mapping' the human terrain, in other words, of going beyond basic cultural familiarity to a more profound level of cultural understanding. The basic philosophy is to counter the bomb-maker in the struggle over ideas, rather than having to counter the bomb itself (Christopher J. Lamb et al., 27). Cultural diversity between

East and West, in our example between the US and Afghanistan / Iraq, leads to many misunderstandings, and Human Terrain Teams (HTTs), at least as they are presented ideally, set out to remedy these misunderstandings and correct the general *naïveté* of other cultures which plagues US forces. Steve Chill, for example, notes: 'Research indicated that many IED [improvised explosive device] attacks were generated as a result of actions that violated sociocultural mores and required violent retribution. Sociocultural understanding was believed to provide a tool to help shape military operations and avoid cultural conflict that spurred violent reaction' (12). There is no consensus on the success of HTTs, given that accurate, objective measurement is difficult and, despite the Army's insistence that Human Terrain Teams are not involved in military intelligence, the participation of civilian social scientists in military operations has raised many ethical questions, especially concerning the informed consent of human subjects and the deontological imperative that no harm be inflicted on the target population. Such critical questions have made their way into contemporary literature, one example being Nadeem Aslam's novel *The Wasted Vigil* (2008), which 'should be read by anyone deploying to Afghanistan,' according to Maximilian Forte. While no mention of Human Terrain Teams appears in the novel, the character of David Town, a culturally-sophisticated gem dealer and former CIA operative, nevertheless functions with the same objectives in mind and confronts the same obstacles. Nadeem Aslam's novel ends on an ambivalent note, as it perhaps must in a context of counterinsurgency, especially if we take seriously David Price's argument that 'once a nation finds itself relying on counterinsurgency for military success in a foreign setting it has already lost,' simply because the entire population has become the enemy (190).[1]

In her Director's message of the Special Issue of the *Military Intelligence Professional Bulletin* dedicated to the Human Terrain System, Colonel Sharon R. Hamilton defines the US Army's Human Terrain System's mission as such:

> The mission of HTS, an intelligence enabling capability, is to: recruit, train, deploy, and support an embedded, operationally focused

sociocultural capability; conduct operationally relevant sociocultural research and analysis; develop and maintain a sociocultural knowledge base to support operational decision making, enhance operational effectiveness, and preserve and share sociocultural institutional knowledge (0).

Clearly, the role of HTS is to support the 'operations' of the brigade to which the team is assigned. The Human Terrain System was the brainchild of General David Petraeus, who famously declared before the US Congress that 'the human terrain is the decisive terrain' (Lamb 1). Mapping the human terrain, according to Petraeus, requires a counterinsurgency approach which focuses on the society and culture of the population and which goes beyond simple cultural awareness, even beyond cultural understanding, to a more profound level of cultural intelligence (Lamb 1; 8).[2] Created in 2006, the first team was sent into the field after training at Fort Leavenworth in early 2007, assigned to the 4th Brigade, 82nd Airborne Division in Afghanistan (Lamb 2).[3] A typical Human Terrain Team is composed of five members, generally including at least one female member: a team leader, a social scientist, a research manager and two analysts, and while those team members who are leading the research project are supposed to have advanced degrees in their field, as we will see this is often not the case. Price, for example, notes that out of a total of over four hundred HTT team members, fewer than eight possess an advanced degree in anthropology (Lamb 14; Price 4). Using knowledge of local populations was of course not new to the US Army. CORDS (Civil Operations and Revolutionary Development Support) had teams in the field during the Vietnam War, gathering ethnographic information which was then used, according to Roberto J. Gonzalez 'to create Phoenix [Program] blacklists. The paramilitary side of CORDS became the prototype for CIA-sponsored death squads' (7). The lessons learned and the sociocultural data that was accumulated seem to have been forgotten after the war, and according to Lamb et al. it was not until the end of the Cold War and the increasing involvement in irregular operations that the US military recognized the ongoing utility of sociocultural knowledge, hence the necessity of data preservation and regular updating as noted in the preceding Director's message (11). Shortly after the first teams were sent into the field in Afghanistan, USCENTCOM (Central Command) approved increasing the programme from an initial trial period of five teams to twenty-six, described by the program's founders as a 'catastrophic success' (Lamb 45; Montgomery McFate and Steve Fondacaro 68). As of Spring 2012, almost all brigades in Afghanistan were equipped with an HTT (Lamb 79). In spite of support from the US military command and generous funding from Congress, the HTS program has not been without controversy, especially as the social and human sciences have, in the past, been tainted by their active collaboration with various colonial projects (Price 14). Other problems include the fact that performance is difficult to measure and has been uneven, as Lamb et al. summarize:

> Many [teams] performed well and earned the approval of the commanders they served, but some failed completely. Performance concerns dogged the program, provoking a number of internal and external reviews and investigations. As a result, there is an amazing amount of colorful secondary literature on Human Terrain Teams, but very little rigorous scholarship on the topic (xiii).

There have, inevitably, been deaths in the field, three between May 2008 and January 2009, including the spectacular case of Paula Loyd, all of which not only creates a negative image in the public mind, but even more significantly, as we see in *The Wasted Vigil*, undermines the Americans' sense of divine mission: 'Every American who dies here, said Casa, dies with a look of disbelief on his face, disbelief that this faraway and insignificant place has given rise to a people capable of affecting the destiny of someone from a nation as great as his' (Lamb et al. 55; *Wasted Vigil* 46).[4] And, perhaps most significantly in terms of scientific methodology, the articulation of civilian social science research with military activities has raised ethical questions regarding observer neutrality and proper deontological procedure when dealing with human subjects. Price cites the Nuremberg Trials as the historical event which provided the discipline of anthropology with its code of ethics, in the wake of Josef Mengele's studies of twins at Auschwitz; Price reminds us that Mengele was, in fact, a physical anthropologist first and a medical doctor second (20-21). Provisions of the Nuremberg Code include: 'scientists studying human beings (in war *and* peace) must obtain voluntary informed consent, must avoid causing mental and physical suffering, must protect research subjects, must use qualified personnel, and must give research subjects the power to end the studies when risks appear' (Price 21). More recently, the American Anthropological Association has published its opposition to Human Terrain Team activities, noting that the respect of the above conditions cannot be assumed in a context of military operations (Price 30). Rounding out the list of problems, the AAA also insists that research and publications generated by HTTs must not be secret (Price 26; Lamb et al. 83; 111), and HTTs have also suffered from difficulties in recruiting qualified personnel, given that recruiting has been outsourced and has 'metastasized into a huge field of sociocultural advisory services without much attention to quality' (Lamb et al. 85). Such is the grey area of mapping the human terrain, wherein we find staunch supporters, virulent critics and everything in between.

The Wasted Vigil is set in contemporary Afghanistan, a human terrain where little or nothing is clearly black and white; suspicions abound, questions go unanswered and although glimpses of truth are found here and there, the 'whole truth' is elusive. The novel cites the CIA motto from the Gospel of John, perhaps not without a hint of irony: '*And ye shall know the truth and the truth shall make you free*' (*Wasted Vigil* 107; original italics). Characters come from Russia, the UK, the USA, Afghanistan, all here as part of the larger context in the aftermath of the Soviet invasion and the global jihad recruited to repulse the godless Communist invaders. One American in particular is interesting in terms of mapping the human terrain: David Town, a former CIA operative and culturally sophisticated gem dealer, who is in Afghanistan seeking a woman named Zameen and her son. David knows the region very well: 'He'd visit Afghanistan's gem mines even during its Soviet occupation when no Americans were permitted. Slipping in from Pakistan and out again without leaving an official footprint anywhere' (*Wasted Vigil* 80), he always remains secretive about his interest in gems: 'David would never reveal anything about the activities hidden behind his gem business, and Marcus knew not to ask, having guessed more or less immediately that he was in espionage' (*Wasted Vigil* 84). As we shall see, David is no longer working with the CIA, having found himself questioning his involvement on moral and ethical grounds, asking the kinds of questions which come up not only among HTT's critics but among team members themselves. Like many HTT recruits, David comes from the Special Forces or the intelligence apparatus (Lamb 135) and, like some HTT recruits, David knows the local culture and language, in this case Pashto (*Wasted Vigil* 122). In spite of being an American, David is able to make connections with the population, hoping to remedy the stereotypical American *naïveté* of other cultures which plagues not only the US military but relations in general between East and West:

> What did they, the Americans, really know about such parts of the world, of the layer upon layer of savagery that made them up? They had arrived in these places without realising how fragile were the defences that most people had erected against cruelty and degradation here. Conducting a life with the light from a firefly (*Wasted Vigil* 134).

HTTs were created out of the recognition that deeper cultural understanding is what was needed in Iraq and Afghanistan, knowing that people like David Town would be able to bridge the cultural gap. The question of how that information would evolve into knowledge and how it would be exploited in terms of policy is of course the central question, both for the fictional characters and for HTTs in the real world.

While the official Army position is that HTTs are neutral, that is, not involved in intelligence, critics argue that HTT neutrality is a fallacy, as it must be whenever social science research is undertaken within the context of military operations. Individual HTT members differ widely in their views of whether their activities are genuinely objective, even as members generally wear a military uniform and some are armed as well (Lamb et al. 61-62). For his part, David Town had come to Afghanistan / Pakistan as a true believer, being both strongly anti-Communist and anti-Islamic extremism, having lost his brother in the Vietnam war and having been present in New York during the first bombing of the World Trade Centre in 1993 (*Wasted Vigil* 112; 85): 'But that was then. By the time he came to Peshawar as an employee of the CIA, his opposition to Communism was the result of study and contemplation. Not something that grew out of a personal wound. He was in Peshawar as a believer' (*Wasted Vigil* 112). Although no longer affiliated with the CIA, David is still a believer, understanding that not only must the enemy—whether Communist or Muslim extremist—be defeated but the community must also be rebuilt. In David's case, he has funded a local school, a gesture which he hopes will contribute to the region's future but which in fact provides a target for a suicide bomber mission, especially since David is an American, an infidel occupier (*Wasted Vigil* 53-54). Human Terrain Teams find themselves in the same quandary, their members participating in the realization of schools and medical clinics and other humanitarian projects, little by little gaining the trust of the local population without ever genuinely succeeding, and sometimes creating and / or becoming targets as well; as outsiders they will never be seen as legitimate (Polk 209-210; Price 187). HTTs may well be a kinder, gentler form of incursion into the local population, but incursion it is, especially when linked to military operations; Price calls it 'a more efficient occupation' (196). The question of how the data from mapping the human terrain will be exploited remains crucial. Whether for the fictional characters in *The Wasted Vigil* or HTTs in the field, credibility is always compromised, and genuine trust is never achieved, largely because of association, past or present, with the military / intelligence apparatus, or as mentioned above simply due to the status of outsider, intruder.

Most would agree that understanding within and between cultures is a good thing in itself; it is the articulation of cultural understanding with military operations which is cause for concern, since civilian scholarship has its own methodology which is often alien to the military / intelligence mindset. Within the novel, David Town's onetime friend and colleague James Palantine plays just such a foil to David's more humanitarian approach to how cultural information should be exploited. James is interested in the same human terrain as David, interested in much of the same information, but drawing different conclusions and using his knowledge to other ends. As Lindsay Beyerstein reminds us, 'Human terrain is analogous to geographical terrain. The same maps can be used to build a bridge or blow one up' (in Price 99). James takes very seriously his role as 'watchman', as elaborated in John Kennedy's undelivered speech, part of which he recalls from memory: 'We in this country […] are—by destiny rather than by choice—the watchmen on the walls of world freedom' (*Wasted Vigil* 204). Suspicious of Casa, James comes to the doctor's house where he'd been given refuge and questions David about him; it must be said that David too is suspicious of Casa while also harboring the idea that he may be Zameen's son. Responding to David's request to leave Casa alone, James replies: 'But this is how al-Qaeda sleeper cells operate in the States. They are like ghosts in front of you, unseen…' (*Wasted Vigil* 282). David nevertheless subscribes to the HTT philosophy of popular support, as described by an unidentified team leader, whereby '95 percent of the bad guys can be brought over' (in Price 112). Although David wins a temporary reprieve for Casa, James will later capture Casa and torture him:

> Casa is on his back on the floor in the centre of the room, his legs being held by an Afghan man, his chest pinned down by the knees of an American who also grips his hands. Another American, beside Casa's head, is holding a blowtorch, its blue jet directed into Casa's left eye. This young man straightens up on seeing David, and just then James comes in through a door on the far side of the room. Casa's mouth is open in a twisted soundless scream, that eye erupting black blood (*Wasted Vigil* 303).

David, working as a civilian and having gained at least partial trust from Casa and others in the area, has unwittingly had his cultural and personal insights appropriated and used by the intelligence community; to James's comments justifying torture, 'It's between them and us,' David demands, 'Have you any idea how much damage you have done *us* by your actions here tonight?' (*Wasted Vigil* 305; emphasis original). Whereas David would prefer ongoing cultural communication and dialogue as a means of conflict resolution, James has opted for torture, two very divergent means of confronting the bomb-maker, thus highlighting the dilemma which most worries critics of Human Terrain Teams. Even though David sincerely tries to avoid violent conflict, he is not completely innocent of compromise either. While working for the CIA, David became aware of a planned Soviet attack on a refugee camp. No one at the CIA, including David, alerted the people in the camp; the attack would be allowed to take place as a means of stirring up anti-Soviet sentiments. Lara learns about this institutional collaboration and is understandably outraged at the logic involved in such a decision:

> [David]: 'The Soviets would have carried out the raid whether or not we knew about it.' [Lara]: 'But you did know about it. That's what I am interested in. God, I had conversations of this type with Stepan ... When it came to what he called his nation, his tribe, he too suffered from a kind of blindness: he saw what he wanted to. 'You think your principles are higher than reality,' he'd say to me.' (Wasted Vigil 290; original italics)

Further illustrating her argument, she wonders aloud whether forgiveness is possible in such a situation, and places her hands over David's nose and mouth, preventing him from breathing; after having made her point, she tells him, 'The forgiveness of the weak is the air you strong ones breathe, David. Didn't you know? You don't see it but you felt it just then. They *allow* you to go on living' (*Wasted Vigil* 291; original italics).

Although a believer, David certainly expresses doubts about his role in Afghanistan, at one point admitting that illegitimate targets were bombed, resulting in civilian deaths (*Wasted Vigil* 239). Another episode also stands out, of a small boy who has just finished his dinner, and in the street in front of his house he is overpowered by two bigger boys, who force him to vomit and then proceed to eat what he has just expelled from his stomach. Barely able to believe what he has just witnessed, David concludes that he 'had helped create all this' before correcting himself: 'No, all this was the Soviet Union's fault because … because … He could not complete the thought' (*Wasted Vigil* 135). Not for the first time does David realize that 'he had been stepping on his own footprints' as he tries to map this particularly complicated human terrain (138). Near the end of the novel, David comes across a citation from *The History of the Decline and Fall of the Roman Empire* which sums up his own dilemma and perhaps that of many HTT members as well: '*The demon of Socrates affords a memorable instance of how a wise man may deceive himself, how a good man may deceive others, how the conscience may slumber in a mixed and middle state between self-illusion and voluntary fraud* (*Wasted Vigil* 288; original italics). Up until the very last, David will try to reason with Casa, the bomb-maker, though to no avail; he had seemed to be making progress, but torture has hardened Casa's resolve. As David tries to pull him from the row of worshippers saying their final prayer before the suicide mission, Casa resists and detonates his bomber's belt. '[David] is hoping to win over his murderer with an embrace. […] The blast opens a shared grave for them on the ground' (*Wasted Vigil* 311-312), and Lara finds herself spattered with the blood of the two men, one from the East and one from the West (*Wasted Vigil* 314). Sociocultural understanding, sought with the methods of counterinsurgency—however enlightened they may be, 'not innocent but […] not guilty'—seems destined to fail and validate the thesis that we have indeed already lost (*Wasted Vigil* 295).

Notes

1. David Price supports his position by citing others as well: Edward Luttwak first, 'Insurgents do not always win, actually they usually lose. But their defeats can rarely be attributed to counterinsurgency' (Price 191; Luttwak 34), and secondly Eric Walberg (himself quoting an unidentified senior French commander), 'If you find yourself needing to use counterinsurgency, it means the entire population has become the subject of your war, and you either will have to stay there forever or you have lost' (Price 191).

2. These three levels of cultural knowledge—awareness, understanding and intelligence—have been suggested as organizational categories which roughly correspond to tactical, operational and strategic levels used by the military. See Lamb 8, and Arthur Speyer and Job Henning, MCIA's Cultural Intelligence Methodology and Lessons Learned, cited in Lee Ellen Friedland, Gary W. Shaeff, Jessica Glicken Turnley, 'Sociocultural Perspectives: A New Intelligence Paradigm,' Report on the conference at The MITRE Corporation, McLean, VA, September 12, 2006, June 2007, Document Number 07-1220/MITRE Technical Report MTR070244.

3. The 50-day HTS Training Curriculum at Fort Leavenworth is organized 'around three core concepts. First, the curriculum is designed to focus on blending civilian analytic expertise with an understanding of military needs and operations. Second, through the use of an educational model that emphasizes practical exercises replicating effective social science methods used to support military operations, the curriculum aims to foster team dynamics and effectiveness while building on social science expertise and fieldwork experience. Third, the curriculum frames social science 'research'[sic] in terms of concepts readily understood by the U.S. military and its coalition partners.' Culture and language instruction are also part of the program. See 'HTS Training and Regulatory Compliance for Conducting Ethically-Based Social Science Research,' by Christopher A. King, Robert Bienvenu and T. Howard Stone, Military Intelligence Professional Bulletin. US Army, October-December 2011. Vol. 37, No. 4. PB 34-11-4, pages 16-17. Original italics.

4. 'Paula Loyd was a member of a Human Terrain Team in Afghanistan when she was doused with petrol and set alight by an Afghan on November 4, 2008. Her attacker was executed while detained [by fellow team member Don Ayla, who was then tried for manslaughter], and she was flown back to Texas for treatment [although she later died of her injuries].' The Unreported Death of Staff Sgt. Paula Loyd of the Human Terrain System: Third Researcher to Die. Maximilian Forte. http://zeroanthropology.net/2009/01/08/the-unreported-death-of-staff-sgt-paula-loyd-of-the-human-terrain-system/ Posted 8 January 2009, accessed 7 October 2014.

8

Historiography and the Question of 'What Happened?'
Uzma Aslam Khan's *The Miraculous True History of Nomi Ali*

On the Acknowledgements page of her 2019 novel, Uzma Aslam Khan tells the reader why she wrote *The Miraculous True History of Nomi Ali*. It was written as a remedy to a largely forgotten chapter of history, namely the prison colony on the Andaman Islands and, more specifically, the women prisoners, who were rarely, if ever, mentioned (371). Although a work of fiction, *Nomi Ali* certainly belongs to the genre of historical fiction, interspersed with citations culled from the archive—diaries, quotes from notable figures of the time, specific dates which correspond to a particular military offensive—and hence able to blur the boundary between history and fiction. This grey area between history and fiction is nothing new, as Keith Jenkins reminds us, since there are always missing elements to the puzzle which are often supplied through conjecture: 'Most information about the past has never been recorded and most of the rest was evanescent,' and of course much of the information that we do possess about the past has been recorded as narrative accounts, in other words presented from a certain point of view and open to disagreement when compared to other accounts (14). If the ultimate goal of *Nomi Ali* is to answer the genuinely historical question, *What happened?* (Khan 322; original italics), then historical fiction has an advantage over the archive, even as it does the work of history (itself a form of storytelling), in being able to fill in the gaps in the historical record, simply because the truth claim is not the same. 'If we are freed from the desire for certainty, if we are released from the idea that history rests on the study of primary / documentary sources [...] then we are free to see history as an amalgam' (Jenkins 58). For historians as well as for novelists, 'every detail is story' (Khan 80), discourses which hope to create meaning within a coherent context, consistent with what one would expect in a given situation, what Lubomír Doležel has called 'possible worlds' (30). Truth, after all, is created, not found (Rorty 3), unsurprising given that we only possess traces and fragments of the past which must then be interpreted and narrativized, which is the goal of historiography: to create a meaningful narrative about the past. *Nomi Ali* does exactly this and, as a work of fiction which becomes historiographical in its 'truthlikeness' (Olivier Laas 1), is freed from truth claims derived from evidence, and thus has the flexibility to fill in gaps and answer questions within a plausible, possible world. 'Art alone,' the dentist Susumu San realizes, 'Could overcome the questions he could not answer' (Khan 164). *The Miraculous True History of Nomi Ali* is a brilliant account of what happened to this society of exiles on the Andaman Islands around the time of World War II and, while there may be other accounts as well, Khan's novel has created a new history and a possible world, using the real world as a notional concept in the same way that an historian uses the past (see Jenkins 79). This new history gives voice to 'those who never got to share their story, who never got to say the words' (Khan 367).

If we can say with certainty that the past has existed, we can also say with the same certainty that the historical record is always incomplete, and can never be otherwise; the past and history are not the same thing (Jenkins 7-8). Even if we limit ourselves to the traces of an event which have—or could have—survived to the present, we enter a contested political terrain, since the dominant power often manipulates historical records in an effort to control the narrative of what happened. *Nomi Ali* foregrounds many such situations, wherein the British and Japanese occupiers falsify or destroy records, or simply gloss over sensitive topics. In school, for example, the children were 'always hungry for real news. The kind Mr. Campbell never spoke of. The kind whispered most often on the island: the freedom movement on the mainland. The teacher would say there was a civil war in Spain and a Depression in America and pretend nothing was happening in India' (Khan 14). The dentist Susumu Adachi, while spying for the Japanese, knows that the historical records he consults as part of his scouting mission are incomplete (Khan 52). And, if the Japanese had wanted to read about the Andamans' geography before their arrival, it would have been impossible to find such a pamphlet, 'as not a single one had been written' (Khan 68). As a spy, Susumu Adachi of course compiles some very complete records and maps of the islands— 'geography, topography, fresh water sources and native tribes'— but expecting his own arrest destroys them (Khan 168). When the prisoners go on a hunger strike to protest the squalid conditions of their detention, they are brutally punished yet 'the incidents could not be reported' (Khan 103). Even prisoner 218D, who managed to escape, was expunged from the prison records to cover up her evasion, such that a journalist named Gill refuses to believe the stories he is told about her heroism, even though Shakuntala offers documentary evidence in the form of a letter. "We've checked all the prison records. She never even came to this island. Most likely, she was an islander. Or a figment of the imagination of a starving people. When the body is stressed, you can never trust the mind" (Khan 358). For someone doing 'pure' history, these kinds of events would never appear, owing to lack of evidence; but, for a writer of historiographical fiction, these absences are an opportunity to tell the story in all of its details: the brutal beatings and rapes, the fear, the hunger, not to mention the "hard to believe" tale of the 'prisoner who was no longer a prisoner' (Khan 357, 323). Although fiction, the 'truth value' or 'truthlikeness' of such literary representations gives them a certain 'epistemological adequacy', in other words, not simply knowing facts but knowing in a certain way, in the case of *Nomi Ali* what Hamish Dalley calls 'ethically engaged interpretations of the actual past' (5), not simply seeking to answer the question 'What happened?' but wanting to do it in a way that gives voice to those who were literally written out of history while at the same time providing an ethical and moral orientation to the narrative.

Answers to 'What happened?' are multiple, and sometimes when no answer can be found the question needs to be changed, or alternatively the answer itself may provoke new questions, and *Nomi Ali* embraces this multiplicity and instability (see Khan 56, 148). Answers are presented in the form of narrative, or discourse, a manner of interpretation which creates meaning (see Jenkins 41), and these discourses - and hence their meanings - 'are always on the move, [...] always being de-composed and re-composed; are always positioned and positioning, and which thus need constant self-examination as discourses by those who use them' (Jenkins 11-12). Several times in the novel, critically-minded characters ask themselves to whom they owe allegiance in this politically contested space, as shown in a dialogue between two local born siblings, Zee and Nomi:

> Mama sides with the British, Baba with the Japanese, whose side are you on?' [Nomi] was stumped. What sort of question was this? Their mother would not be here if not for the British, she had been forced, it was called transportation for life, just because Zee was already in her stomach when Baba did what he did. [...] 'That makes no sense,' she decided. [...] And she has wondered ever since, ever since, why she did not think to ask, What's our side, Zee? (5).

Throughout the novel, a scene from Aunty Hanan's dream is recollected as well, further illustrating the difficulty of knowing what course of action to take: '*If that strange long-haired boy in the pointy boat keeps heading for the island, it is the wrong choice; but retreating is not the right one either*' (116, 154; original italics). When questioned about the freedom movement and the armed resistance of some of its members, Kaajal asks Aunty Hanan, "Were they brave or were they wrong?", to which she replies, "They were both" (228). Nomi also undergoes what might best be called mystical experiences, whereby she splits in two, seemingly able to experience an event first hand while at the same time seeing herself do so as a distant observer: '[Nomi] began to separate. One half of her stood still, watching the other half become everything she had ever seen' (181). Nomi's father too has a recurrent dream, wishing as he does for a second chance: 'That egg in his dream, it was always there. He could not get to it, but it was there, as though to offer a parallel truth, one in which things could start all over again. He had only to smash the bottle without hurting the egg' (Khan 191). These characters struggle with the instability of the answers which can be hard to pin down with any certainty, and they agonize over choices past and present which have an effect on how the situation evolves. Aye, for example, wonders whether he should have saved his 'one favour' from Loka to save the prisoner 218D (151), or to save Zee. He is also torn between choosing to save Nomi or her mother from drowning at sea (303-304). As we have said, a fiction writer is better able to get inside the heads of his/her characters, expose their motivations, desires, beliefs and fears, and thus relate information generally unavailable to the historian. Yet *Nomi Ali* deals with this psychologizing in a very interesting way, highlighting the fact that making the right choice can be difficult, even impossible, and that there are multiple perspectives which foreground the idea that there may be no single answer, but instead parallel truths. Like the historian, the novel writer may also acknowledge the philosophical problem of 'other minds,' as elaborated by Ludwig Wittgenstein: 'If one has to imagine someone else's pain on the model of one's own, this is none too easy a thing to do: for I have to imagine pain which I *do not feel* on the model of pain which I *do feel*. That is, what I have to do is not simply to make a transition in imagination from one place of pain to another' (§ 302; original italics). The conclusion, as Jenkins reminds us, is that we are fundamentally unable to enter the mind of someone else, no matter how empathetic one may be, and this is further linked to Croce's dictum that 'all history is contemporary history,' meaning that entering another's mind is even more difficult given that historiography speaks about the past but from the perspective of the present (48-49). *Nomi Ali* is a work of fiction and, as such, the author is free to disregard this problem and invent 'other minds'. Yet the use of multiple perspectives, difficult if not impossible choices, and answers regarding what happened which are not fixed, seem to suggest that the problem of 'other minds' is taken very seriously, and as such helps to give the novel a strong historiographical aspect.

Nomi Ali is a historiographical fiction of exiles and, despite literature's reputation of often romanticizing exile, Edward Said's warning regarding twentieth-century exile is clear:

> [T]hat exile is irremediably secular and unbearably historical; that it is produced by human beings for other human beings; and that, like death but without death's ultimate mercy, it has torn millions of people from the nourishment of tradition, family and geography[.] (138)

Exile is central to the question, What happened? on the Andaman Islands, and *Nomi Ali* also seems to reply to Said's question, 'Are [the experiences of exiles] not manifestly and almost by design irrecoverable?' by doing exactly that, recuperating the stories of these exiles (139). Although the Andaman Islands were intended as a penal colony, especially to house the large number of prisoners taken by the British after the 1857 Mutiny (Dalrymple 425), we see that the experience(s) of exile are multiple, although the prison, shaped like a starfish (37), maintains its centrality. Prisoners were of course transported, served their time and—if they survived—were released, and then perhaps founded a family and thus created a new generation of local born children who knew no other homeland. Prisoners' families were transported with them, as we have seen with Zee and Nomi, both born on the island because their mother, pregnant with Zee, was forced to accompany her husband. Some chose exile, like Shakuntala, who was married to a British administrator living in India:

> I grew up with hate,' [Shakuntala] tried again, softly. 'Between my parents. Between Hindus and Christians. Between Indians and the British. Between myself and my in-laws. Between myself and my mother and then her father, who had nothing good to say about mine. It is hard to explain, but when you grow up between so many worlds, something changes. It is why I came here. To get away from all that hate. And your father and I found on this rock a way to love each other, in peace. Here of all places (332).

For Shakuntala, exile is 'better than staying behind,' having grown up between too many worlds (Said 141). The historical context of *Nomi Ali* is set around World War II, most importantly the growing independence movement in colonial India, and the war itself, especially the Japanese occupation of the Andaman Islands, supplanting the British. Of course, none of the occupiers were appreciated by the indigenous islanders. In other words, the Andaman Islands became a geographic proxy for competing nationalisms—British imperial expansion, Japanese imperial ambitions, Indian nationalism—and Said reminds us that nationalism and exile must be considered together. 'Informing and constituting each other', as they do, 'both terms include everything from the most collective of collective sentiments to the most private of private emotion, there is hardly language adequate for both' (140). Once again, we might suggest that historiographic fiction is exactly the right medium to describe and share the often-private experiences of exile, the kinds of experience which don't generally leave a trace in official archives.

Exiles are aware of at least two cultures, 'and this plurality of vision gives rise to an awareness of simultaneous dimensions, an awareness that—to borrow a phrase from music—is *contrapuntal*' (Said 148; original italics). Characters in the novel are victims of '*Deracination. Dislocation. Dissociation*' (Khan 183; original italics) and, as such, possess exactly this plurality of vision and awareness of simultaneous dimensions, perceiving a home culture, occupiers' cultures, as well as indigenous knowledge, capable of understanding the messages carried by various kinds of winds (61, 294), for example. Given that his father is a convict, and that he is a local born under British occupation, Zee tends to speak English and works hard at school in hopes of obtaining a scholarship to study in Britain. Rather than see his father as a role model, 'Zee looked instead to his teacher, an Englishman. It was always Mr. Campbell this, Mr. Campbell that. [Zee's father] could not read or write English' (Khan 30). Yet Zee's father, having lived under occupation in India, thinks otherwise: 'Zee would have to learn, soon enough. He would have to see the wrong in believing in those

HISTORIOGRAPHY AND THE QUESTION OF 'WHAT HAPPENED?' 103

that wronged them' (30). Aye too, although local born, is affected by a past which he did not experience first-hand:

> When Aye's great-grandfather first came to these shores on the Darya-e-Noor in 1858, he had been told it was to a place where men and women would forever be separated from every possession held hear. But what was left of the living with the death of the past? The ship had been the bridge between the living and the dead. She was both a bad and a good nat, tearing him from one world and guiding him to the next. Afterwards, she had disappeared, to herself become a ghost (Khan 147; original italics).

With a past largely dead, the victim of exile very often finds that going home is no longer an option (see Said 142). The opportunity does indeed arise, as the war nears its end and the British have now re-occupied the Andaman Islands after the Japanese, and the overseer Andrew Gallagher 'wonder[s] if the local population had suffered enough. Was it time to pardon the prisoners and their children, the Local Born? Should they be awarded the choice of repatriation to the mainland, or continued residence on the islands?' (Khan 326). Yet many of the exiles choose to stay, once again illustrating the difficult, sometimes impossible, choices that must be made. Nomi's mother, for example, refuses to leave, because her son, Zee, 'was buried here. His blood had made a home of this soil' (Khan 361). Shakuntala too plans to remain, 'This was her home' (Khan 267), and many of those who do leave for the mainland in fact return:

> In the coming months and years, many of those who could leave would do so only for a short time, to bring a little dirt from mainland India and mix it with the dirt here, to stake a claim, finally, to this *zameen*, this land, as belonging to them. Nomi hoped, one day, to do the same. She would go to Jalandhar, her father's home, bring back its earth, link it with Andaman earth, and their story would, in some small way, be safe (Khan 361).

In an ironic twist of historical fate, the Andaman Islands, after so many years' service as a violent penal colony, would become a refuge for exiles fleeing the violence of Partition in 1947, thus creating another cycle of those for whom the past would die and become like a ghost (Khan 367, 368).

Nomi Ali, this historiographic novel of exiles, creates an alternative, possible world which, while fiction, may indeed be true. Said insists on the legitimacy of the novel as such, saying: 'The novel [...] exists because other worlds *may* exist' (144; original italics). While a historical narrative may claim a certain 'referential truthfulness' (Laas 11) that a novel does not, *Nomi Ali*, being historiography, may indeed make at least a partial referential claim to historical veracity, as we have said, genuine historical events like the experiments testing quinine as a remedy for malaria in the Islands, which left many dead (64; 144). Yet as fiction, the novel is free to create a possible world; Laas, paraphrasing Doležel, makes the distinction between world-imaging texts and world-constructing texts: 'I-texts are representations of the actual world and provide information about it. The world itself exists prior to and independently of I-texts. C-texts are the results of world-making practices that construct the worlds represented in them. Such texts exist prior to the world they describe' (11; see Doležel 24). This possible world has been created in an attempt to answer the question, What happened?, and since the available archival traces do not allow us to have a complete answer to that question, *Nomi Ali* supplies us with a possible answer, or more precisely with what Laas calls 'a certain set of potential answers [...] In historiography, answers can be construed as explanations of hypotheses [...] as well as strategies for drawing further inferences from the answers' (20), arriving at what Karl Popper called 'a *better approximation to truth*' (335; see Johansson 2; original italics). Much like Aye's gift of a carved wooden hen to Nomi, 'untrue' in a real-world sense yet not implausible, '[Aye] had never seen a hen like it, but hoped she would find that this did not make it wrong' (Khan 148), the truthlikeness of *Nomi Ali* makes it entirely legitimate to assert itself as a possible answer, or set of answers, to the question 'What happened?' Since the novel's time frame spans about ten years, from 1936 to 1947 (although characters look retrospectively to before 1936), it takes the reader through evolving possible worlds, and explicitly allows the characters to seek other possible worlds as they try to navigate difficult choices and ambiguous answers. After Kaajal's death, the prisoner who was not yet a prisoner wonders 'why they kept asking for one answer, when they knew as well as she did that freedom was made of many parts' (Khan 221). *The Little Mermaid*, rather than *A Doll's House*, becomes the model for young girls' dreams of another, possible world:

> That day, Kaajal explained that the little mermaid's tale was truer to what was happening in India, and possibly all over the world, where most women were not slamming doors but choosing between identities. 'Do you know the story? The mermaid wanted what she could not have. Most people think the object of her love was a human being, but that was not all. The object of her love was another world.' [...] 'She was given legs to enter the other world, but at what cost? She lost her community. She became neither mermaid nor human. It is the saddest story I know, and sometimes I feel we're in it, girls who fall in love with freedom (Khan 218).

Seeking to enter another, unknown world, but at the cost of exile, of losing one's home, what Said calls 'the tragic fate of homelessness in a necessarily heartless world' (146), such is the price that the Little Mermaid has had to pay. During the Japanese occupation, Aye tells himself that he must 'walk into another future he could not know' (Khan 289) as he prepares to flee to a forced labour camp: '*Stand up!* said the father wind, rising now to its full height, dwarfing the rock on which it had once sat. *Stand up and receive this world again!*' (Khan 294; original italics). Aye, a Burmese local born (9), possesses the multiple cultural knowledge mentioned earlier, including indigenous knowledge, which allows him to listen to what the wind and the island have to say.

Historiography is a way of making sense of the past, constructed in a meaningful way so that a community can make a history their own, 'a history that is aware of what it is doing' (Jenkins 45, 82), hoping to create a space 'for the desirable outcome of as many people(s) as possible to make their own histories such that they can have real effects (a real say) in the world' (Jenkins 81). Jenkins goes on to say that such histories 'can make visible aspects of the past that have previously been hidden or secreted away; that have previously been overlooked or sidelined, thereby producing fresh insights that can actually make emancipatory, material differences to and within the present—which is where all history starts from and returns to' (81). It is this point, that history/historiography is written in and for the present—a history is 'always for someone' (Jenkins 21)—and, while Jenkins is speaking of innate bias in how a historical event is narrativized, in the case of *Nomi Ali* it seems reasonable to suggest that this particular history was also written *for* those whose stories had never been told. As a truthlike representation of a possible world, this novel, by answering the question 'What happened?', makes an implicit assertion, a possible answer, not only in terms of the events that are described, but by how that description is oriented morally and ethically, given what we know about war, empire, exile, and the many other cruelties that human beings have visited on one another. This hindsight can indeed, according to Jenkins, allow us to 'know more about the past than the people who lived in it. In translating the past into modern terms and in using knowledge perhaps previously unavailable, the historian discovers both what has been forgotten about the past and pieces together things never pieced together before' (15-16). Nomi and Aye, for example, become focal points of this world of exiles, link people to a lost world, because 'the world still did not look here' (Khan 367):

> The longer Aye cupped the cranium in his hands, the more he understood why he had been saving the prisoner's letters. It was as though through them he had found a few scraps of a disappeared world, even a disappeared father. This man whose bones he held—his life, his spirit, it had to rebone itself. The letters and bones were a link to a lost world for a people who were lost. In his hands, the people were somehow linked (Khan 147).

Nomi too tries to fill in the gaps of the story, rummaging through scraps of paper, hoping to find traces> 'When Aye saw her uncrumpling the paper, he reminded her that the Japanese had destroyed all the records of their occupation, and destroyed many of the jail records, too. After the British reoccupied the island, they had taken away whatever they could find. [...] But Nomi said that if the Japanese could leave the staircase, they might have left other things, maybe without even knowing it, things the British too never found' (Khan 365). These exiles' lives, their spirits, are recuperated through historiographical fiction, as they have left no trace in archives, have left no evidence behind, and as we have seen, without evidence such stories are hard to believe. Their stories are all connected, as part of the answer to What happened? prisoner 218D, Aye and Nomi: '[Aye] did not appreciate the extent to which fate had connected them, perhaps from the very day that she stepped off the S.S. Noor. She had looked at him and, separately, at Nomi on her way up to the jail. One day, he and Nomi would remember this' (Khan 322-323). When asked, What happened? Aye would tell of the hundreds of people pushed off boats to drown, others shot, while most who survived those massacres would starve (Khan 322). A memorial was built to honor their memories and their stories, where survivors burn paper with names of the dead, 'a reminder that there were those who never got to share their story, who never got to say the words. Perhaps it was for this reason that Nomi kept looking for lost words in the scraps in the rubble in Mr. Howard's villa' (Khan 367). By blurring the boundary between history and fiction, *Nomi Ali* tells the story of what happened to these exiles on the Andaman Islands, truth likeness in the context of a plausible, possible world, and thus is able to give voice to those who have gone unrecognized in official historical archives. As perhaps a better approximation of truth than 'pure' history, the novel wears its title well, The Miraculous *True* History of Nomi Ali.

PART 4 | MIGRATION

9

Exit West

The Making of a World

Mohsin Hamid's recent novel, *Exit West* (2017), addresses the issue of forced migration, a societal issue which always seems to be current. According to the UNHCR, the United Nations Refugee Agency, in 2017 68.5 million people were migrating, many millions not by choice (Satoshi Sugiyama). *Exit West* is a good example of the 'worlding' of Pakistani literature in English, grounded as it is in a certain time and place (let's call it Pakistan) yet which could be almost anywhere, anytime. Locations may, or may not, be specified, yet the reader identifies with the characters' plight in spite of geographic ambiguity. As politically-engaged literature which has something to say about the real world, the novel transcends the boundaries of its country of origin, and becomes more than Pakistani literature, resonating far beyond local issues, implicating humanity on a much broader canvas. A review of the novel in *The New Yorker* offers the same appraisal: '[*Exit West*] feels immediately canonical, so firm and unerring is Hamid's understanding of our time and its most pressing questions' (Jia Tolentino). Much of the research on world literature, starting with Goethe's comments on the subject,[1] has tended to focus on the circulation of 'great' works of literature, which are then translated into many languages or read in the lingua franca of English and consumed by the cosmopolitan elite. David Damrosch's *What is World Literature?* (2003) is a significant contribution to the idea of world literature as moving from national to international contexts and, while these definitions of world literature as international circulation are interesting, they tend to overlook more profound questions of capitalist globalization and the ways in which world literature can function as a political tool, providing ethical orientation in a world which world literature also helps to create. Pheng Cheah's *What is a World? On Postcolonial Literature as World Literature* (2016) is an excellent addition to the debate on the active role of world literature, which attempts to answer some of the more profound questions which arise, beyond the frequently Eurocentric definition offered by Goethe. In Cheah's words, his book:

> explores how the conceptualization of the world in temporal terms provides a normative basis for transforming the world made by capitalist globalization and how this normative understanding of the world leads to a radical rethinking of world literature as literature that is an active power in the making of worlds, that is, both a site of processes of worlding and an agent that participates and intervenes in these processes (2).

When considering a theory of normativity, Cheah has in mind not simply literary circulation in the global marketplace, but rather:

> seeks to understand the normative force that literature can exert in the world, the ethicopolitical horizon it opens up for the existing world […] temporalization constitutes the openness of a world, the opening that is world. In situations where, progressive teleological cartographies are leveled off by capitalist globalization, this openness is an unerasable normative resource for disrupting and resisting the calculations of globalization […] without this opening that puts all beings into relation, we would not have access to other beings and no value could be formed (5; 9).

Temporalities must of course be considered in the plural, as Cheah suggests, because a world is composed of 'multiple temporalities' which have been subjugated by global capitalist linear time (symbolized by Greenwich Mean Time, not coincidentally located in the UK), resulting in the incorporation of 'peoples outside the European world-system by violently destroying their worlds […] The survival of these worlds is necessary to the constitution of a larger world of humanity that is truly plural' (12). Mohsin Hamid's *Exit West* assumes a political role within these more complex definitions of world literature, given that it is 'a form of critical resistance that brings the attention of the wider world to the plight of peoples impacted by global forces and their struggles to safeguard a future for their worlds' (Cheah 17). While Cheah proposes many theoretical lenses with which to examine postcolonial literature as world literature, for the purposes of this chapter three points have been chosen which can be applied to *Exit West*, with the goal of offering some critical questions for reflection, a starting point for further research: natality, storytelling, and postcolonial literature as world literature.

In the novel, doors are the pathways to new worlds, and passing through these doors is represented as a birth; the door is 'the heart of darkness. And out of this darkness, a man was emerging [...] He wriggled with great effort, his hands gripping either side of the doorway as though pulling himself up against gravity, or against the rush of a monstrous tide. [...] With a final push he was through, trembling and sliding to the floor like a newborn foal' (6-7). Later in the novel, it is the protagonists, Saeed and Nadia, who pass through a door for the first time, the image of twin births as they enter a new world:

> It was said in those days that the passage was both like dying and like being born, and indeed Nadia experienced a kind of extinguishing as she entered the blackness and a gasping struggle as she fought to exit it, and she felt cold and bruised and damp as she lay on the floor of the room at the other side, trembling and too spent at first to stand, and she thought, while she strained to fill her lungs, that this dampness must be her own sweat. Saeed was emerging and Nadia crawled forward to give him space... (98).

Cheah cites Hannah Arendt, who insists on the priority of natality in 'The Concept of History,' and its constant injection of newness into the existing world, a world wherein new entries are born into the game which has always already begun: 'Human action, like all strictly political phenomena, is bound up with human plurality,[2] which is one of the fundamental conditions of human life insofar as it rests on the fact of natality, through which the human world is constantly invaded by strangers, newcomers whose actions and reactions cannot be foreseen by those who are already there and are going to leave in a short while' (Arendt 61, qtd. in Cheah 137). According to Cheah, Arendt then expands her notion of natality to a more metaphorical level, that of 'initiation,' suggesting that all human activities 'contain an element of initiation' (Cheah 137). 'All human activities,' Arendt goes on to say,

> are relays of natality. They introduce three types of newness into the world and the unpredictability that accompanies the emergence of the new. First, the birth of any human being is the beginning of something new in the existing world that disrupts deterministic causal chains. Second, the introduction of new objects into the fabricated world is metaphorically likened to birth. These objects become another factor that conditions human life. Third, the fact of plurality means that other new subjects will be born into the world. Each entry changes the world and gives rise to actions on the part of existing subjects that also change the world. The persistent coming of new others intensifies the unpredictability of actions and their outcomes, leading to greater variability in the human-made conditions that shape our lives (Cheah 138).

Exit West describes community meetings/gatherings in similar terms, highlighting the notion that human activities, however routine, often represent a metaphorical birth or an initiation:

> Deliberations were often slow and cumbersome, so these gatherings were not particularly thrilling. And yet Nadia looked forward to them. They represented something new in her mind, the birth of something new, and she found these people who were both like and unlike those she had known in her city, familiar and unfamiliar, she found them interesting, and she found their seeming acceptance of her, or at least tolerance of her, rewarding, an achievement in a way (Hamid 145).

Continuing the metaphor of birth, a re-birth via migration is generally a one-way voyage; in spite of migrants' initial intentions of one day returning to their country of origin, for many reasons, the return trip is often impossible, or at least undesirable, as the protagonist Nadia explains:

> [Nadia] wondered whether she and Saeed had done anything by moving, whether the faces and buildings had changed but the basic reality of their predicament had not. But then around her she saw all these people of all these different colours in all these different attires and she was relieved, better here than there she thought, and it occurred to her that she had been stifled in the place of her birth for virtually her entire life, that it's time for her had passed, and a new time was here, and fraught or not, she relished this like the wind in her face on a hot day... (Hamid 156).

Diversity and newness are other ways of describing what Arjun Appadurai has called 'uncertainties,' and *Exit West* argues that diversity and uncertainty are not simply to be accepted but encouraged. A society which is far too homogeneous and sure of itself is an intolerant, indeed violent, society as it struggles to remove uncertainty in the context of globalization:

> [...] globalization exacerbates these uncertainties and produces new incentives for cultural purification [...] large-scale violence is not simply the product of antagonistic identities but that violence itself is one of the ways in which the illusion of fixed and charged identities is produced, partly to allay the uncertainties about identity that global flows invariably produce (Appadurai 7).

Nadia understands that, given the choice, an uncertain society, with all of its potential for an open-ended future, is preferable to a society which is absolutely certain of its identity; a closed society may be easier to manage, but stifles its citizens by considering 'new' as the enemy.

Our second point, storytelling, is related to the first in that storytelling is a narrative repetition, the 'generation of meaning by remembrance of the past' (Cheah 151). Most humans cannot remember their own births, with the exception of enlightened individuals like the Buddha who are apparently able to recall all of their previous incarnations, yet those who are re-born through migration have the benefit of memory, not only living their own stories but able to recall them and transmit them to others, a re-telling which then has effects of its own, as Arendt suggests: 'Narration is a recounting that connects different stories into a larger whole in which 'the unique life story of the newcomer' affects 'uniquely the life stories of all those with whom he comes into contact'" (Arendt, *Human Condition* 184, qtd. in Cheah 151). The other obvious benefit of storytelling, especially in written form, is the ability to outlive both the actors in the world and those who tell their stories, and becomes part of the plurality of stories which are continuously being 'added to the world's stock' (Cheah 153-154).[3] A human lifetime is short, even in the best of circumstances, and such human fragility is a central theme of *Exit West*, as one example from the novel shows, a 'new born' migrant who reflects: 'Growing up in the not infrequently perilous circumstances in which he had grown up, he was aware of the fragility of his body. He knew how little it took to make a man into meat: the wrong blow, the wrong gunshot, the wrong flick of a blade, turn of a car, presence of a microorganism in a handshake, a cough. He was aware that alone a person is almost nothing' (Hamid 7). Many of the stories that circulate in the novel are transmitted through the technologies of modernity: portable telephones, social media, television news. 'In their phones were antennas, and these antennas sniffed out an invisible world, as if by magic, a world that was all around them, and also nowhere, transporting them to places distant and near, and to places that had never been and would never be' (Hamid 35). While Saeed tries to limit his time on social networks, Nadia consumes those stories without constraint: 'She watched bombs falling, women exercising, men copulating, clouds gathering, waves tugging at the sand like the rasping licks of so many mortal, temporary, vanishing tongues, tongues of a planet that would one day too be no more' (Hamid 37), once again an acknowledgement of the fragility of human beings and the necessity of storytelling as a means of leaving a trace for posterity, if indeed there would be a posterity. Stories related by television news are described as 'apocalyptic,' although, as we will see, the lived experience of these migrant newcomers and the natives is, though difficult, less than apocalyptic. 'Outside the house much was random and chaotic, but inside, perhaps, a degree of order could be built. Maybe even a community. There were rough people in the house, but there were rough people everywhere, and in life roughness had to be managed. Nadia thought it madness to expect anything else' (Hamid 129). Even a suicide attempt is aborted by a man who chooses to believe the stories he has heard of doors leading to better places, placing his hope in an uncertain future, and succeeding (Hamid 127-128).

Finally, the question arises, how does a work of postcolonial literature, *Exit West* in our example, become part of world literature, beyond the fact that it is written in the lingua franca of English or translated into other languages and widely circulated by an international publisher? According to Cheah,

> In Arendt's vocabulary, it is a matter of disclosing and announcing through stories the experiences of a given people as a collective actor that is part of a shared world being destroyed by globalization. At the same time, this disclosure must also account for the problematic character of national collectivity in relation to disadvantaged minority groups and how the nation is interminably dislocated and reconstituted by various global flows Cheah 211).

The novel describes just such a situation in microcosm, wherein the migrants are moving, 'in the manner of cards dealt from a shuffled deck during the course of a game, reassembling themselves in suits and runs of their own kind, like with like, or superficially like with superficially like, all the hearts together, all the clubs together, all the Sudanese, all the Hondurans' (Hamid 142-143). Arendt herself tells us, in *Was ist Politik?*, 'The world comes into being only if there are perspectives; it exists as the order of worldly things only if it is viewed, now this way, now that, at any given time [...] Human beings in the authentic sense of the term can exist only where there is a world, and there can be a world in the proper sense of the term only where the plurality of the human race is more than a simple multiplication of copies of a species' (Arendt 105-6; 175-176; qtd. in Cheah 194). Decolonization, and the stories of decolonization, are part of a political agenda to 'open up a world that is different from the colonial world', an ongoing project 'in light of the inequalities created by capitalist globalization and their tragic consequences for peoples and social groups in postcolonial space' (Cheah 194). Minorities, Appadurai reminds us:

> are a recent social and demographic category, and today they activate new worries about rights (human and otherwise), about citizenship, about belonging and autochthony, and about entitlements from the state (or its phantom remnants). And they invite new ways of examining the obligations of states as well as the boundaries of political humanity, falling as they do in the uneasy gray area between citizens proper and humanity in general (42).

Minorities also remind a society of its failed promises to produce fair and just government, and indeed call into question the image of purity itself, as minorities' his/stories recall past violence in the creation of the state (Appadurai 42). A world, according to Cheah, should be 'the endless process of opening itself' (192). *Exit West* takes into account the necessity of leaving the doors open, describing situations which accept the arrival of newcomers and the inherent instability of permanent migration; after all, even if one never moves, the world around us does. At one point in the novel, the authorities in London are planning to raid the migrant camp, but abandon the idea:

> Perhaps they had decided they did not have it in them to do what would have needed to be done, to corral and bloody and where necessary slaughter the migrants, and had determined that some other way would have to be found. Perhaps they had grasped that the doors could not be closed, and new doors would continue to open, and they had understood that the denial of coexistence would have required one party to cease to exist, and the extinguishing party too would have been transformed in the process, and too many native parents would not after have been able to look their children in the eye, to speak with head held high of what their generation had done (Hamid 164).

Near the end of the novel, the Bay Area of California also becomes a space of transition, where 'the apocalypse appeared to have arrived and yet it was not apocalyptic, which is to say that while the changes were jarring they were not the end, and life went on, and people found things to do and ways to be and people to be with, and plausible desirable futures began to emerge, unimaginable previously, but not unimaginable now, and the result was something not unlike relief' (Hamid 215-216). Newcomers will continue to arrive in a world that precedes them, a world which then depends on their arrival to perpetuate itself, and their life-stories which are then told and retold adding to the archive, the differing perspectives that constitute our world in spite of apocalyptic prognostications, will continue to orient our moral and ethical compass and test our political fortitude as we imagine a world of open doors.

Notes

1. In the Introduction to What is World Literature?, David Damrosch cites Goethe, who is speaking to his disciple Johann Peter Eckermann in January 1827: 'I am more and more convinced that poetry is the universal possession of mankind, revealing itself everywhere and at all times in hundreds and hundreds of men ... I therefore like to look about me in foreign nations, and advise everyone to do the same. National literature is now a rather unmeaning term; the epoch of world literature is at hand, and everyone must strive to hasten its approach' (1).

2. Rosa Ruela, in an article about the integration of Ismaeli Muslims in Portugal, quotes the President of the Ismaeli Council of Canada, Malik Talib: 'Diversity is a fact, pluralism is a choice' (16). My translation.

3. Hannah Arendt, in The Origins of Totalitarianism, makes an interesting correlation between the homeless refugee and a 'merely biological human being,' in other words a human being who has lost his/her humanity in being reduced to a biological entity, a move which paradoxically affects what have been called universal human rights (as defined by the United Nations, for example), such that, according to Cheah, 'the very gesture of endowing the human being with naturally given, inalienable rights ironically deprives him of his humanity and worldliness, the human capacities for action and speech that create a meaningful world' (Arendt 302, qtd, in Cheah 157). See also Arjun Appadurai, 'minorities are a recent social and demographic category, and today they activate new worries about rights (human and otherwise), about citizenship, about belonging and autochthony, and about entitlements from the state (or its phantom remnants). And they invite new ways of examining the obligations of states as well as the boundaries of political humanity, falling as they do in the uneasy gray area between citizens proper and humanity in general' (42).

10

Snuffing Out the Moon

Kino/Bio Politics, Movement and the State of Exception

Osama Siddique's debut novel, *Snuffing Out the Moon* (2017), is (to paraphrase Mohsin Hamid) a migration through time, and like the Buddha 'travelling through multiple lives on the road' (Siddique 18), is set across four millennia in the Indus Valley, moving between eventful periods in this region's history: 2084 BC (The Land of the Indus), 455 CE (The Land of the Buddha), 1620 (The Land of the Mughal), 1857 (The Land of the Sahib), 2009 (The Land of the Wakeel) and finally 2084 (The Land of Tomorrow). Shifting between these six different historical eras in South Asia, Siddique charts the politics of movement. As in Hamid's *Exit West*, much of the migration is politically motivated: as Thomas Nail insists, 'the migrant is the political figure of movement' (11). Mohenjodaro, a beautiful model city, is falling into ruin because of decadence and a caste of priests who have usurped religion from the people and turned it into a political weapon, which, accompanied by natural catastrophes, forces exodus. The Land of Tomorrow sees the globe divided into competing Water Conglomerates amid 'the growing number of Displaced and Migratory Persons' (254), leading to war and the desertion of warriors to the camp of the Regressives, hoping for a simpler, more meaningful life, rather than remaining in a society where travelling to the past is forbidden. Civilian populations and monks taking to the road in 455 CE in an effort to survive, both physically and spiritually, the onslaught of invading hordes: 'A new people had arrived and they would murder and pillage for so long that no house would resemble a human dwelling and courtyards with calm images of Lord Buddha would look like slaughterhouses' (367), transforming forever the society from what it had been. During the Indian Mutiny of 1857 and the cataclysmic social mutations which resulted, Mahmood prays for courage in the coming fight: '[T]he everyday terms of existence were far from illusory. They lived real lives. Increasingly uncertain lives. The old order was in its last throes and a new one stood by the side of the deathbed' (42). Whether on the level of an individual or of an entire society, 'the social compulsion to move produces certain expulsions for all migrants' (Nail 2), exclusions of those who are seen as a threat to national identities and national economies because they fall outside the social orders which seem to guarantee the disciplined bodies and minds which are the basis of biopolitics described by Foucault and others. When confronted with such existential threats and resistance, real or imagined, a sovereign often resorts to emergency measures, what Moira Fradinger, after Agamben and Schmitt, calls a 'zone of exception,' wherein the border between legal and illegal becomes blurred: 'The law legally suspends itself, in order to preserve itself. A lawless space is thus legally bound: its violence is rationalized by the rhetoric of constituency survival and temporarily tolerated by the legal institutions' (Fradinger 17). Those who move are forced into this grey zone, both inside and outside the law; *Snuffing Out the Moon* traces four millennia of history, showing that the state of exception, rather than being 'exceptional' or temporary, instead seems to be a permanent means to consolidate power, and that kinopolitics, or the politics of movement, is at the centre of biopolitics (in Foucault's sense, namely of socio-political power over individuals and communities) and at the centre of the state of exception as well.

As Nail makes clear, 'the figure of the migrant has always been the true motive force of social history' (7), and Siddique's novel lends itself to a kinopolitical approach to historical evolution. The novel, divided into five 'books', each containing six historical periods, opens with a description of Mohenjodaro, 2084 BCE, a thriving, vibrant city along the mighty Indus river, traders coming and going

- in short, a model city, which gives the impression of permanence, of always having been there. Yet, if the primary basis of kinopolitics is the 'analysis of social flows,' a secondary feature is the junction, or perceived stasis:

> But this relative stasis is always secondary to the primacy of the social flows that compose it. A junction is not something other than a flow. It is the redirection of a flow back onto itself in a loop or fold. [...] The junction then acts like a filter or sieve that allows some flows to pass through or around the circle and other flows to be caught in the repeating fold of the circle (Nail 24; 27).

Seen from this perspective, it becomes clear that a city like Mohenjodaro at some point had to be created through movement, thus making Nail's claim unambiguous, that in fact, 'settling down is the first kinopolitical event' (39). Given the vocabulary of social flows, it is perhaps not a coincidence that water imagery is abundant in *Snuffing Out the Moon*. And indeed, Mohenjodaro is literally being drowned by heavy rains since its infrastructure has not been maintained due to the laxity of civic leaders since a fraudulent priestly caste has taken power. One young man, Prkaa, disgusted with the charlatans who have corrupted his city, is living in exile in the nearby forest; as an exile, or one who has been expelled, Prkaa is deprived of social status, 'resulting in, or as a result of, [...] movement' (Nail 35). Whether Prkaa has chosen exile or been expelled ultimately does not matter, since 'migrants [...] are not free to determine the social conditions of their movement [...] Expulsion is a fundamentally social and collective process because it is a loss of a *socially* determined status (even if only temporarily and to a small degree)' (Nail 36; original italics). Prkaa, though treated by the city dwellers as a barbarian, as one who is outside the political order (Nail 15), is not naïve; he understands that the decline of the once-great city is due to the priests who have taken power, priests who are referred to as 'illusion-makers' (138).

In the novel, we are told that organized religions developed out of fear, becoming 'a framework for tackling all the terrors of the unintelligible and the unknown' (Siddique 155), and evolved into a system of socio-political exploitation meant to control human beings, perfectly in line with Foucault's definition of biopolitics, and reminding ourselves that a 'junction' is necessary to organized religion, a community of people living together and believing together (see Nail 155):

> Religion could no longer be left to mere men. It enfolded a possibility too immense to ignore any more, it encapsulated a tool too ingenious to neglect. […] it was only a matter of time before priestly persuasion evolved into exhortation and then into diktat. […The priests] required obeisance. They required submission. They even required a sacrifice no less than freshly shed blood. […] The officiators of the new religion increasingly thought it fit to play a cardinal role not just in the domain of the spiritual but also in that of state, politics, commerce and even in the private lives of men and women. And who was to question them? (Siddique 156-157).

Even when their hoax is exposed and the voice of 'god' revealed to be a man hiding in a tree, this caste of sovereign priests which has been sacrificing human beings manages to remain in power, so successful have their 'technologies of the self' been, whereby 'processes of subjectivization bring the individual to bind himself to his own identity and consciousness by the city dwellers and, at the same time, to an external power' (Agamben, *Homo Sacer* 5), or what Foucault called docile bodies. If the creation of subjects is necessary to the sovereign, the state of exception too is not a pre-existing situation, but rather the means by which this caste of sovereign priests 'creates and guarantees the situation that the law needs for its own validity' (Agamben, *Homo Sacer* 17), within this society facing an apparent state of emergency, the aforementioned torrential rains and flooding.

2,500 years later, in the Land of the Buddha, the city of Mohenjodaro has all but disappeared under the sands of time. In the city of Takshasilla, the monks have settled in the Jaulian monastery, whose ruins will, in their turn, form the backdrop for the Deep History Centre 1,600 years hence. A senior scholar, Buddhamitra, is reproaching his brothers for their sedentary habits, remaining in the sangharama when the tradition of the Buddha was to 'go forth into the world' (23), adding: 'the wheel of time takes yet another turn and the world around us is changing. [...] Surely, we need to be aware of what is happening beyond the walls of our monastery? Whether we like it or not, events transpiring outside can disrupt our quiet, reclusive lives within...' (23). The outside is simply moving in, as it always does. Buddhamitra is not simply worried about religious tradition; he has been having visions of invading hordes wiping out their current civilization (124), and taking to the road will be their only hope for survival, both for themselves and for the message of the Buddha which they carry. And so the monks will become exiles, although they take it in their stride as the normal functioning of the wheel of time, or in the terms of kinopolitics, as the motive force of history: 'Civilizational existence was nothing more than the tiresome sequence of horde after horde crossing deserts or descending from mountains, persecuting and uprooting those who had settled and flourished in the plains, only to be displaced in turn by the next series of marauders' (Siddique, 311). Two forms of kinopolitical movement are appropriate to this kind of situation, according to Nail: the invading hordes are nomad barbarians who 'engage in one continuous raid following only the flows of blood and treasure—always searching for a home denied to them by political disenfranchisement' (138), while the monks become refugees, seeking asylum with their brothers in a distant monastery (see Nail 135). The permanence of movement also becomes clear. If earlier we mentioned junctions as the points of perceived stasis, we now enter a system of circulation, or a 'regulation of flows into an ordered network of junctions' (29), wherein the migrant (in whatever form, whether nomad, exile, refugee...) never really arrives at a destination (see Nail, 245 endnote), especially given that invasions of one kind or another are a permanent feature, indeed a driving factor, of history. Agamben links the phenomena of insurrection, invasion, resistance and such to the state of exception, highlighting the paradox that while the state of exception might seem to apply to abnormal, exceptional situations, within the concept of "global civil war," the state of exception tends increasingly to appear as the dominant paradigm of government in contemporary politics' (Agamben, *State of Exception* 2). Siddique's novel argues along the same lines, yet, takes us well back from contemporary history to show that such techniques of government are nothing new, and will probably not change in future societies either.

In 1620 CE, The Land of the Mughal, we find Manmohan taking to the Shah Rah-e-Azam, the grand road 'on which rode those who shaped their own destinies and indeed those of empires. Soon, he too would walk on it to escape a life of crushing tedium' (25). As a young son to a large, poor, farming family, Manmohan is a mere subject, a vagabond forgotten by history; the historical figure is Emperor Jahangir, The Seizer of the World, a genuine sovereign with effectively no limits to his power (see *State of Exception*, 8). Jahangir is a conqueror who has dramatically expanded his empire, what Nail refers to as a centripetal force, and:

> In this way, territorial kinopower *collectively* brings the outside in. Thus, neither expansion nor expulsion is the effect of a single or central ruler, law, or power. Centripetal force does not emerge from the centre; it emerges from a decentred periphery. It is the kinetic conditions for a social centre. A single centre can be created only by slowly accumulating from a heterogeneous periphery of individual farmers and even multiple territories (43; original italics).

Nail highlights the problem, saying that the migrant has been understood historically from the 'perspective of *states*,' in other words by those who have written the historical record, narratives in which the simple farmers and foot soldiers like Manmohan are ignored (4; original italics). But, of course, empires also come and go.

Another major historical event highlighted by *Snuffing Out the Moon* is 1857 and the Indian Mutiny, the state of exception par excellence declared by the East India Company and the British Crown; rebellions, Nail reminds us, 'are about seizing power directly without fleeing' (147). The British blame an itinerant maulvi, Ahmadullah Shah, who 'had travelled across northern Hindustan, inciting rebellion wherever he went' (Siddique, 109), and the British are concerned as well by the mystery of travelling chapattis across the country, which are suspected of being coded messages and which, disconcertingly, are delivered much more quickly than the post (see 104). When considering rebellions, Nail refers to the wave as the most appropriate form of motion to describe this kind of social movement:

> A wave transports a qualitative change or *social force* of solidarity or collective disruption. [...] A social wave simply transports a disturbance through a social collective that unifies the collective without the source of the transport originating from any single point. [...] Social revolt travels rapidly in between the formal channels of power, through 'word of mouth,' print, association, and all manner of viral underground communications and secret meetings. Thus, a social wave is a distinctly mass or *common* phenomenon that requires a multitude of *mutual* pedetic motions in order to transmit a social disturbance among heterogeneous elements (127).

Even though the Indians refuse to move, their rebellion consists of movement nevertheless, the kind of Brownian movement described above. During this time of social upheaval, many travelled figuratively as well as literally underground, in elaborate systems of tunnels: 'There was some comfort that all of them—whether stately or mean—almost always harboured those who were fleeing something and that too in great haste; an equalizing of humanity when it was underground, not unlike the egalitarian state in which all found themselves sooner or later, whether concealed in elaborate crypts or in dusty, untended graves' (203). The British make prisoners of many of the Indian soldiers and civilians, all of whom are assumed to be guilty by association, and whose lives mean nothing, and their bare life status can be read on their bodies: 'For they were men in limbo, moving about like wayward spectres in the twilight. [...] They looked like debased men, and they walked like debased men, their eyes were those of debased men...' (Siddique 289). Later in the novel, more prisoners are taken, but will not remain prisoners for long: 'The stragglers were to straggle no more. Such was the order. There was to be a blanket and permanent ban on all their movements. Now such a ban could only be truly implemented on lifeless bodies...' (393). These people are to be killed—but not sacrificed—because they are stragglers, because they cannot move fast enough, because they cannot keep up.

In the context of a large-scale social revolt such as the Indian Mutiny, Nail describes the genesis of such resistance, what he calls the 'holy trinity of proletarianization (expulsion from property, urban labour and biological fecundity)' which then 'gave birth to the social movement' allowing local struggles to evolve 'into social and national struggles. [...] the proletariat became the propertyless majority and their motion became a larger *social* movement' (159; original italics). Although the resistant Indian seems motionless in his/her refusal to move, in fact s/he continues to do so, moving 'together in the picket-line, the public demonstration, the occupation....' (Nail 172). As we have seen, the self-proclaimed sovereign, in this case the East India Company and the Crown, reacts by repression, arrests with indefinite detention and killing, using the most basic logic to justify the state of exception, that of 'necessity,' which, Agamben reminds us, 'has no law' (*State of Exception*, 24), ultimately destroying through martial law and emergency powers the very democracy (albeit limited) which the state of exception was supposed to defend, simply because there are no limitations on the exercise of power, no system of checks and balances (see Carl J. Friedrich 584; see also Agamben *State of Exception* 8). While Indian independence was still ninety years in the future, the Mutiny was nevertheless a significant challenge to the sovereign, and indeed the East India Company found itself divested of that role, replaced entirely by the Crown.

Contemporary Lahore is the setting for the chapters entitled Wakeel, highlighting an old woman who is the victim of weak institutions and corruption. A gang of strong men has occupied her house and refuses to pay rent, while the lawyer who is supposedly representing her case is simply taking her money while colluding with her tormenters. She is bound to, and yet abandoned by, the law (see *State of Exception* 1). The law has become weak, as Agamben, citing Walter Benjamin, insists, 'If the awareness of the latent presence of violence [which both posits and preserves the law] in a legal institution disappears, the juridical institution decays' (Benjamin, 144; see also *Homo Sacer,* 40). When the legal system becomes weak, like a watchdog which barks incessantly but never bites, the door is left open to those who understand that there are more efficient ways of governing than democracy and respect for the law, and such is the case as a senior Army General decides to take power through a coup d'état: 'General Sahib had decided that no longer could the fate of the nation be left to the civvies [...] *General Sahib was a man of action and had little patience for the law.* [...] *General Sahib was a man of action and had even less patience for history*' (Siddique 267-268; original italics). Although Al-Wakeel is one of Allah's ninety-nine names—The Trustee, The Disposer of Affairs, The Guardian—Wakeel can be defined linguistically as 'the person who efficiently represents him [sic] or does what he is incapable of doing on his behalf' (Understand al-Qur'an, n.p.). While the old woman eventually finds an honest lawyer to represent her, perhaps more important to our discussion in terms of kinopolitics is the man who takes pity on the woman and steps in to help. The man, Billa, is an outlaw himself, fleeing for his life yet, before leaving his hideout, he becomes the figure of Robin Hood, the sort of popular vagabond myth of the highwayman which Nail suggests, 'supports peasant struggles, disguises himself as a beggar, hates the clergy, and fights the sheriff and his men' (150). In the current context of a military dictatorship, led by a sovereign General who has little patience for the law, the old woman has not completely lost her legal status yet requires someone from outside the law to defend her against the injustices of the state of exception and weak legal institutions (see *State of Exception,* 3).

Snuffing Out the Moon also takes us to the future, although not that far off, in 2084, to a world divided into competing Water Conglomerates. The Rohtas Fort Encampment is ultramodern and technologically advanced, kept secure by Airborne Monitoring and Patrol Scooters flown by skilled pilots. Every so often, one of the patrols manages to take a long-distance picture of those who are exiles, called Regressives by the city dwellers as they 'seemed to belong to another age' (60). One of the pilots, Naya, is curious about these people, and wonders why photos of them are so rare, and why 'the Regressives were hardly spoken about. They were simply out there. Except when they needed to be checked' (61). The photos are on display in the Fort, until one day when Naya's close-up pictures of a family were also posted and caused quite a sensation, at least until they were censored a few minutes later—the man in the Regressive family is wearing the same kind of military-issue trousers that all AMPS pilots wear (63). Thus, he is not simply an exile, but a deserter, an extremely politically-charged form of movement or migration. Nearly four years earlier, Combat Specialist Prashanto went missing after a seek-and-destroy missionand was ultimately classified as Missing in Action (84) after his AMPS inexplicably crashed in the jungle while pursuing some Regressives caught trying to divert water from the Conglomerate for their own use (79). Now that Naya's photos have unintentionally identified Prashanto, the authorities order an immediate recovery mission, classified as Code Red and Confidential, with the addendum *'Damnatio Memoriae'*— no record is to be made of the operation (75), as a means of avoiding any martyrization. 'Didn't one know how icons were born? If one neglectfully allowed a mythos to develop around someone or something, it became almost impossible to contain it at a later stage. 'The Burning Man,' 'The Tank Man,' 'The Falling Man,' 'The Passion of the Che'... various iconic images from some time earlier in the century flashed through [the Resident Reviewer's] fast-paced mind' (74-75). The Water Conglomerate has become a totalitarian society, controlling information and discouraging those who wish to consult the historical archive, dismissed as 'the countless fabrications fed to people over millennia in the name of a discipline that used to be called history' (62).

Prashanto, discussing why he left the Conglomerate to live with the Regressives, explains why he was unhappy:

> The loss of perspective has resulted from the forced break with the past—a horribly gory and death-dealing past by all accounts, but there is an absolute restriction on excavating it, examining it, learning from it—except for the select few. We are supposed to live solely in the present and in the future. So that the contagion

of the past does not deprave us. The past is a curse that we are
supposed to have escaped. It can never be allowed to catch up with
and degenerate those who have, through their endless toil, finally
regenerated. It is the necessary damnation of memory, some say. But
how can one live without memory? (230).

In terms of kinopolitics, this interdiction to travel to the past is really nothing new, as Nail reminds us; those in power have always had power over the historical archive too, including the 'countless fabrications' cited earlier:

…Migrants have created very different forms of social organization
that can clearly be seen in the 'minor history' of the raids, revolts,
rebellions, and resistances of some of the most socially marginalized
migrants. This is a challenging history to write because many of
these social organizations produced no written documents, or if they
did, they were systematically destroyed by those in power. It is not
a natural fact that the history of migrants has become ahistorical,
as Hegel argues—it is the violence of states that has rendered the
migrant ahistorical (4-5).

In this violent society, where religious faith has been banned in favour of 'the cult of science and the order of progress' (232), water scarcity has become a political tool, indeed a weapon of war (252) which has pushed many into exile, not simply those called Regressives:

In the wake of the Water Wars and after the so-called 'Transformation,'
children, women and men had gone forth in caravans, small and
large, clinging together for fear of persecution, and direly in need
of water and security. After the stabilization of the extant global
power balance among the Conglomerates, their places of exile
became semi-permanent abodes. The reasons for their ouster were
multifarious. Many had been turned away because they were deemed
incapable of conforming; others had refused to conform and attune
themselves to new post-religion lives. Yet others were born while
their parents were in exile and know of no other life […] they all
had something in common—their collective rejection by those who
now controlled the water reserves of the world (233).

There is nothing new in this kind of expulsion, Nail suggests: 'The social conditions for the expansion of a growing political order (including warfare, colonialism, and massive public works) were precisely the expulsion of a population of barbarians who had to be depoliticized at the same time. This occurs again and again throughout history' (23). Such expulsion does not happen from a pre-established territory, in this case the Conglomerates' zones of influence and walled forts, rather territory is created via the expulsion of those who stand in the way: 'The territory is not the condition for movement, but the inverse. [...] Before there is the territory, there is a process of territorialization' (Nail 42).

As we have said, travelling to the past is strongly discouraged in this society; only near history studies are valued (Siddique 238). Alexander Al-Murtaza Afaqi was once a contemporary history specialist, renowned in his field, until he began to have doubts about what he was doing, and about what ideological purposes his work served. So he is sent to the Deep History Studies Centre in Taxila, where, in the shadow of the ruins of the Jaulian monastery, he is allowed to do his research, knowing that he is being monitored and that his work will at best be censored (236-240). Taxila is where Alexander Al-Murtaza Afaqi and people like him are confined when they are seen as 'Not yet volatile or seditious to qualify for surgical or chemical reorientation' (240). Knowing his work will never be published, he is currently working on the history of the Indus Valley civilizations, and the central role of water, then as now, in their respective cultures, millennia apart, (241). Naya too, since her unwitting discovery of a deserter to the camp of the Regressives, is being subjected to questioning and scanning, treated as though she were a threat to the security of the Conglomerate, and is being considered for memory erasure. She wonders aloud, 'What kind of authority system played havoc with memory? What kind of society tolerated it without a word of explanation, without any disclosure? What did the authority have to hide and why?' (246-247). During his interrogation with the Resident Reviewer, Alexander shows clearly that he understands the bio-political justification for altering memory, defining it simply as 'the age-old project of enforced normalization' (251). Both he and Naya will rebel; Alexander will leave microchips hidden inside several different statues, records of his writings that were not revealed to the Conglomerate, hoping that the historical archive will travel to the future without being destroyed as subversive (425), and in the last lines of the novel Naya will bail out of her AMPS to join the Regressives below, as Prashanto had done four years earlier (427). While defined as deserters by the Conglomerate, and hence as criminals deserving of the death penalty—'*killed and yet not sacrificed*', according to Agamben (*Homo Sacer* 8; original italics)—Nail suggests that what Prashanto, Naya and the Regressives have accomplished is yet another form of social movement, that of the commune which 'proposes an alternative to the state' (167). The commune is, thus, a 'wave invention of the proletariat' (Nail 167), the wave provoking a qualitative change in society, as was mentioned above, becoming a 'permanent way of life' (Nail 139). As the Water Conglomerates seem to be in a constant state of conflict, both with each other and internally, security remains a top priority, thus justifying the state of exception and the resulting 'generalization of the paradigm of security as the normal technique of government' (Agamben, *State of Exception* 14).

Snuffing Out the Moon, abundant with water imagery is, as we have said, about migration through time and the social flows which drive history. At one point, Prkaa seeks answers from his teacher: 'I often wonder whether a civilization can always progress [...] The more I think about all this, the more I am convinced that the affairs of men sometimes follow a course that becomes irreversible. It is like a tide which, once it rises, abates only when the natural time for it to abate arrives' (334). Prkaa is pessimistic about the possibility of a small group of people changing the tide of history for the better, and his pessimism is understandable. Those social flows, or movements of peoples, are almost never random but instead the result of political pressures: expulsions and expansions, invading armies, marauding hordes, imperial projects, exiles and desertions. If bio-politics is the creation of docile bodies for the purpose of controlling people and ensuring normalization, kinopolitics must be considered as a means of accomplishing much the same thing, through enforced, regulated movement. As part of this constellation of governance, we see that the state of exception, rather than being the result of an exceptional situation is in fact the necessary element which defines the sovereign, allowing the sovereign to then reduce human beings to bare life, both inside and outside the law, permitting 'both to protect life and to authorize a holocaust' (Agamben, *Homo Sacer* 3). We also see that, unlike some theorists who present the state of exception as a relatively recent historical phenomenon, Osama Siddique's *Snuffing Out the Moon* suggests that the exception has been the rule for thousands of years. Invoking necessity allows the sovereign to define memories, to create collective amnesia, to rewrite history. Yet, throughout *Snuffing Out the Moon,* there are those who are nostalgic, curious, seeking to escape 'the order of things' (41), trying to see beyond appearances (15), those who doubt. Prkaa's teacher replies to his question: 'This city may falter, fall and wither away. Or it may not. But those capable of building one such as this will not die out. We too will survive' (335). If movement is a tool of social control, it is also a means of resistance, of escape, of survival.

11

'Eventful' History, Movement, and Social Mutation

Possible Futures

William H. Sewell, in his book *Logics of History: Social Theory and Social Transformation*, argues for a theoretical engagement between social theory and history, focusing especially on events which can radically alter social structures. Using Wallerstein's world system, rather than the nation-state, as his model of structure, Sewell contends, 'An eventful concept of temporality assumes that contingency is global [...] Contingent, unexpected, and inherently unpredictable events, this view assumes, can undo or alter the most apparently durable trends of history' (102). Societies are sites of overlapping structures which govern human conduct, and structural transformation on a small scale can result in new values and meanings being attributed to larger, older categories, implying that both local and global transformations may result from the same causes (Sewell 85-6). As we have seen in much Pakistani and Kashmiri writing, considered as historical fiction and social critique, the genuine event is often the pattern of migration / movement on large and small scales—whether caused by conflict and war, Partition, economic instability or environmental catastrophe—and contingency is the arrival of newcomers whose presence will force a reassessment and ultimately a transformation of existing structures, of values, of human conduct. But eventful history is still history, and as such is told as a story, as White reminds us:

> No set of real events, even those comprising an individual life, displays the kind of formal coherency met with in what we

conventionally recognize as a story. We may seek to give our lives a meaning of some specific kind by telling now one and now another kind of story about them. But this is a work of construction rather than of discovery—and so it is with groups, nations, and whole classes of people who wish to regard themselves as parts of organic entities capable of living story-like lives (*Fiction* 230).

Meaning is imposed on such stories, according to White, given that narratives are often classed in categories such as tragedy, comedy, satire and such, thus already orienting the reader to interpret the event / story in a certain manner (*Fiction* 230).

Sewell discusses three temporalities employed as theoretical lenses by historians and social scientists, beginning with teleological temporality, informed by the notion of progress: Although no longer as popular as it was in the 19th century, with a declining belief in the inevitability of universal progress, teleology has proved resistant as a theoretical framework. The second temporality which Sewell highlights is comparative historical analysis, or experimental temporality, an approach championed by Theda Skocpol, which is a useful analytical tool 'when there are too many variables and not enough cases' (Skocpol 36; cited in Sewell 91). Skocpol used comparative analysis to examine the French, Russian and Chinese revolutions, events which, although rare, nevertheless allowed comparison in ways that Wallerstein's world-system, being unique, does not. Finally, the theoretical approach which is most appropriate to our current objects of study, eventful temporality, which 'takes into account the transformation of structures by events' (100). Structures and events are not mutually exclusive, as it might first appear, but depend on one another in several ways. Sewell credits Marshall Sahlins, a structural anthropologist, for his work recognizing their articulation, and summarizes thus:

> Events, in Sahlins's reformulation, are transformations of structure, and structure is the cumulative outcome of past events. Sahlins points out that events are recognizable as such only within the terms provided by a cultural structure. Events can be distinguished from uneventful happenings only to the extent that they violate the expectations generated by cultural structures. [...] Moreover, what

consequences events will have depends on how they are interpreted, and that interpretation can only be made within the terms of the cultural structures in place (199).

While there may be some disagreement regarding whether a specific happening should be regarded as an event, especially since events are interpreted within a given social structure, it is the consequences of the event which must be highlighted, and whether the resulting transformation / transition is significant on a large scale, by violating cultural expectations, which distinguish an event from a more routine incident. White also underlines these moments of transition and the resulting problems of representation: '...a 'transition' is precisely what *cannot* be represented in any medium (even cinema) because it is what happens 'between' two states considered to be (relatively) stable: it is the moment of the 'switch,' the moment of the 'trans-substantiation' in which the 'wine' of one historical reality suddenly 'becomes' the 'blood' of another' (*Fiction* 305; original italics). White's remarks could be tempered in relation to the primary texts under consideration in the preceding study, to suggest that fiction is perhaps the medium best suited to represent moments of transition, or in light of the politically engaged nature of these works to encourage such transformation of structures. A major event can often be primed through more humble means, such as promoting a broader historical consciousness among the audience, filling in the gaps in the historical record with a story that might be true.

To Wallerstein's capitalist world-system must be added a more political perspective regarding large-scale structures, that of Michael Mann in his four-volume *The Sources of Social Power*, and his assertion that those social structures which can be called 'civilizations' (defined by Sewell as 'the cluster of innovations that includes cities, writing, states, extensive division of labour, and permanent social stratification', 115) emerge only with systematic oppression, or what Mann called the 'social cage.' 'Civilisation,' according to Mann, 'was a complex whole of insulating and caging factors' resulting infrequently over long periods of time, and only when systematic oppression could be permanently installed (74).

Sewell, paraphrasing Mann, explains why so many societies came close to becoming civilizations without ever actually doing so:

> ...The monarchs or chieftains in such social orders lacked the power resources to impose enduring authority over their subordinates or to establish systems of stratification that permanently denied resources to the less favoured categories. This is because the ruled normally had the option of *escape* from the emerging authority relations, either by physical flight to areas beyond the would-be despot's control or by switching their loyalty to an alternative chief who would offer them better conditions. Unless the subordinate groups could be physically caged, prevented somehow from moving elsewhere when disgruntled, the systematic oppressions without which civilization was impossible could not develop (116; original italics).

Sewell supports Mann's macro-historical approach as emblematic of eventful temporality, as it highlights global contingency within social processes which, Sewell reminds us, 'are inherently contingent, discontinuous, and open-ended'. Big and ponderous social processes are never entirely immune from being transformed by small alterations in volatile local processes. Such contingency, such open-endedness when dealing with human beings and their societies do not follow simple mathematical formulas or physical laws, so that, according to Sewell, 'adequate eventful accounts of social processes will look more like well-made stories or narratives' (111). As we have seen among the many well-made stories previously discussed, Soniah Kamal's *An Isolated Incident* illustrates the plurality of histories, and the necessity of one story to be completed by others, exactly the kind of plurality that totalitarian societies refuse to admit (White, *Fiction* 106). Mirza Waheed's *The Collaborator* also brings a traumatic past and present together in a very material way, in a very specific place, the Kashmir Valley. While political solutions certainly exist, the novel leaves us pessimistic about possible futures available to these people. In *The Upstairs Wife*, Rafia Zakaria blends history and memoir, highlighting the micro-histories that are always a part of macro-history, and the need to understand their articulation in a holistic manner. So, too, with the 'then and now' of Basharat

Peer's *Curfewed Night,* which also insists on the personal / political nexus in lived experience. Communities are made up of individuals, after all, just as individuals can barely be said to exist outside these communities. Mohsin Hamid's *Filthy Rich* continues along these lines, showing the catastrophic outcomes for both individuals and societies when self-help is taken to its neoliberal limits and solidarity is lost. Pakistan and Kashmir have, as has been said, gone through an eventful history, much of it traumatic: Partition, the 1971 civil war, the Afghan war, and so on, events which have often quite literally changed the landscape, including the human terrain, as we have seen in Nadeem Aslam's *The Wasted Vigil,* and the consequences of cultural appropriation and efforts to control the dominant narrative. *Nomi Ali* also does so, Uzma Aslam Khan delving into the archive to discover what was missing from the narrative, and proposing a plausible story to fill in the gaps and answer the question of what happened. *Exit West* is an eventful account of social evolution and structural transformation, all due to magical doors that allow immigrants / emigrants to quickly move from one place to another through unofficial channels, destabilizing the status quo to such a point that these doors and the resulting migration 'were being discussed by world leaders as a major global crisis' (Hamid 83). These world leaders are of course alarmed by the prospect of unchecked global mobility. If we recall the above-mentioned definition of civilization, which insists on an oppressed, immobile underclass. These doors allow escape, and in a very literal sense, threaten civilization itself—at least, as understood by the dominant class. Osama Siddique's *Snuffing Out the Moon* takes us through four thousand years of movement in the Indus Valley, showing that major events and societies in motion are nothing new in the historical process, yet insisting that such movement is never random but always a reaction to an event as a means of physical and cultural survival, although s/he who moves is often ostracized as political motives come into play. The preceding novels and memoirs are full of depictions of the status quo, of what typically happens when migrants are seen as a threat to cultural purity and fixed national identity; *Exit West,* for example, describes a situation wherein 'nativist extremists were forming their own legions, with a wink and a nod from the authorities, and the social media chatter was of a coming night of shattered glass' (132), a clear allusion to *Kristallnacht*, the anti-Jewish pogrom carried out by Nazi authorities and civilians in 1938, marking the beginning of the Final Solution, the Nazi version of utopia. The novels and memoirs in the preceding study call for spaces of transition and transformation, unimaginable previously, as we have said, because constrained by structural conditions—recall Mann's social cage—but not unimaginable now that structures are being transformed by the event of permanent, global migration as well as movement on a more local, more personal scale. Migrants and other newcomers will continue to arrive, not in static, pre-existing communities but in communities that were also created through the movement of peoples and cultures, and all of the differing perspectives will continue to constitute our world in spite of apocalyptic prognostications and resistance in the name of national and cultural purity, proving that civilization outside the cage is not only possible but desirable, and ultimately absolutely necessary.

Works Cited

Agamben, Giorgio. *State of Exception*. Translated by Kevin Attell. Chicago: University of Chicago Press, 2005. Originally published as *Stato di eccezione*. Torino: Bollati Boringhieri editore s.r.l., 2003.

———. *Homo Sacer: Sovereign Power and Bare Life*. Translated by Daniel Heller-Roazen. Stanford, CA: Stanford University Press, 1998. Originally published as *Homo sacer: Il potere sovrano e la nuda vita*. Giulio Einaudi editore s.p.a., 1995.

Ali, Mehrunnisa. 'General Mohammed Ziaul Haq's Visit to Muslim Countries.' *Pakistan Horizon* Vol. 30, No. 3/4 (1977): 103–7. <http://www.jstor.org/stable/41393337> Accessed 25 May 2013.

Altounian, Janine. *La survivance: Traduire le trauma collectif*. Préface de P. Fédida, postface de René Kaës. Paris: Dunod, 2000.

Altounian, Janine. *De la cure à l'écriture : L'élaboration d'un héritage traumatique*. Paris: Presses Universitaires de France, 2012

Appadurai, Arjun. *Fear of Small Numbers: An Essay on the Geography of Anger*. Durham and London: Duke University Press, 2006.

Arendt, Hannah. *The Human Condition*. Chicago: University of Chicago Press, 1958.

Arendt, Hannah. 'The Concept of History: Ancient and Modern,' in *Between Past and Future: Six Exercises in Political Thought*. New York: Viking Press, 1961. 41- 90.

Arendt, Hannah. *The Origins of Totalitarianism*. San Diego, CA: Harcourt Brace, 1973.

Arendt, Hannah. *Was ist Politik? Fragmente aus dem Nachlaß*, ed. Ursula Ludz, Munich: Piper, 2003, 105-106, translation modified; 'Introduction into Politics,' in *The Promise of Politics*, ed. Jerome Kohn, New York: Schocken, 2005, 175-176.

'A Sensible Call: Haj Sermon.' *Dawn*. 16 October 2013. Accessed 17 October 2013. <http://www.dawn.com/news/1049971/a-sensible-call-haj-sermon>. Accessed 17 October 2013.

Asia Society, ed. *Asia's Next Challenge: Securing the Region's Water Future*. New York: Asia Society, 2009.

Aslam, Nadeem. *The Wasted Vigil*. New York: Alfred A. Knopf, 2008.

Badruddin, Asad. 'A Muslim Majority Indus Valley Civilisation?' *Dawn*. 22 June 2012. <http://www.dawn.com/news/728611/a-muslim-majority-indus-valley-civilisation> Accessed 4 April 2013.

Ballard, Roger. 'The Political Economy of Migration: Pakistan, Britain, and the Middle East,' in *Pakistani Diasporas: Culture, Conflict, and Change*, ed. Virinder S. Kalra. Oxford in Pakistan Readings in Sociology and Social Anthropology, ed. Ali Khan. Oxford: Oxford University Press, 2009, 19–42. Originally published in *Migrants, Workers, and the Social Order*, ed, Jeremy Eades. London: Tavistock, 1987.

Bauman, Zygmunt. *Modernity and Ambivalence*. London: Polity, 1991.

Benjamin, Walter. 'Zur Kritik der Gewalt.' In Benjamin, *Gesammelte Schriften*, vol. 2, I. 'Critique of Violence.' Trans. Edmund Jephcott. In Walter Benjamin, *Reflections*, ed. Peter Demets. New York: Schocken Books, 1978.

Bergson, Henri. *Creative Evolution*. 1911. Trans. Arthur Mitchell. Mineola, NY: Dover, 1998.

Beyerstein, Lindsay. 'Anthropologists on the Front Lines.' *In These Times*. 30 November 2007.

Bobin, Fréderic. 'La rivalité sunnites-chiites au Pakistan, un des défis du future premier ministre.' *Le Monde*. 11 mai 2013. 4.

Butt, Nadia. 'Inventing or Recalling the Contact Zones? Transcultural Spaces in Amitav Ghosh's *The Shadow Lines*. *Postcolonial Text* Vol. 4, No. 3 (2008): 1-16. <http://postcolonial.org/index.php/pct/article/viewFile/869/627> Accessed 11 July 2015.

Butterfield, Herbert. *The Historical Novel: An Essay*. Cambridge: CUP, 1924.

Casey, Edward. *Imagining: A Phenomenological Study*. Bloomington: Indiana University Press, 2000.

Cheah, Pheng. *What is a World? On Postcolonial Literature as World Literature*. Durham and London: Duke University Press, 2016.

Chellaney, Brahma. *Water: Asia's New Battleground*. Washington DC: Georgetown University Press, 2011.

Chill, Steve. 'One of the Eggs in the Joint Force Basket: HTS in Iraq/Afghanistan and Beyond.' *Military Intelligence Professional Bulletin*. US Army, October—December 2011. Vol. 37, No. 4. PB 34-11-4. 11-15.

Dalley, Hamish. The Postcolonial Historical Novel: Realism, Allegory, and the Representation of Contested Pasts. New York: Palgrave Macmillan, 2014.

Dalrymple, William. *The Last Mughal*. London: Bloomsbury, 2006.

Damrosch, David. *What is World Literature?* Princeton and Oxford: Princeton University Press, 2003.

Doležel, Lubomír. *Heterocosmica: Fiction and Possible Worlds.* Baltimore and London: Johns Hopkins University Press, 1998.

Doležel, Lubomír. *Possible Worlds of Fiction and History: The Postmodern Stage.* Baltimore: Johns Hopkins University Press, 2010.

Doran, Robert, ed. 'Introduction.' In *The Fiction of Narrative: Essays on History, Literature, and Theory 1957-2007.* Baltimore: Johns Hopkins University Press, 2010.

Dufour, Dany-Robert. *Les mystères de la trinité.* Paris: Gallimard, 1990.

Eswaran, Mukesh, Ashok Kotwal, Bharat Ramaswami and Wilima Wadhwa. 'Sectoral Labour Flows and Agricultural Wages in India, 1983-2004: Has Growth Trickled Down?' *Economic and Political Weekly* 44 (2): 46-55.

Flusser, Vilém. *The Freedom of the Migrant: Objections to Nationalism.* Tr. Kenneth Kronenberg. Ed. Anke K. Finger. Urbana, Chicago and Springfield: U of Illinois P, 2003.

Forte, Maximilian. http://zeroanthropology.net/2009/05/07/whitewashing-a-us-war-crime-in-afghanistan-the-trial-of-don-ayala-human-terrain-mercenary/ Posted 7 May 2009, accessed 3 September 2014.

Foucault, Michel. *Discipline and Punish: The Birth of the Prison.* Trans. Alan Sheridan. New York: Vintage, 1977.

Fradinger, Moira. *Binding Violence: Literary Visions of Political Origins.* Stanford, CA: Stanford UP, 2010.

Freud, Sigmund. *Malaise dans la civilisation* (1929). Paris: Payot, 2010.

Friedrich, Carl J. *Constitutional Government and Democracy.* Second edition. Boston: Ginn, 1950. Originally published Boston: Little, Brown & Company, 1941.

Gaborieau, Marc. 'Islam and Politics.' *A History of Pakistan and its Origins.* Ed. Christophe Jaffrelot. London: Anthem Press, 2004. 237-251.

Gayer, Laurent. *Karachi: Ordered Disorder and the Struggle for the City.* Oxford: OUP, 2014.

Gledhill, John. 'Official Masks and Shadow Powers: Towards an Anthropology of the Dark Side of the State.' *Urban Anthropology* 28 (2): 199-251.

Gonzalez, Roberto J. *American Counterinsurgency: Human Science and the Human Terrain.* Chicago: Prickly Paradigm Press, 2009.

Gupta, Akhil. *Red Tape: Bureaucracy, Structural Violence, and Poverty in India.* Durham and London: Duke UP, 2012.

Halbwachs, Maurice. 'La doctrine d'Emile Durkheim.' In *Revue philosophique* 85, 1918. 353-411.

Halbwachs, Maurice. *Les cadres sociaux de la mémoire.* 1925. Paris: Albin Michel, 1994.

Hamid, Mohsin. 'Why Pakistan will Survive.' *Pakistan: Beyond the Crisis State.* Ed. Maleeha Lodhi. London: Hurst & Company, 2011. 35-43.

Hamid, Mohsin. *How to Get Filthy Rich in Rising Asia.* New York: Riverhead Books/Penguin, 2013.

Hamid, Mohsin. *Exit West.* Hamish Hamilton / Penguin Books, 2017.

Hamilton, Sharon R. 'HTS Director's Message.' *Military Intelligence Professional Bulletin.* US Army, October-December 2011. Vol. 37, No. 4. PB 34-11-4. Pages 0 and 3.

Hanif, Mohammed. *A Case of Exploding Mangoes.* London: Jonathan Cape, 2008.

Hegghammer, Thomas. *Jihad in Saudi Arabia: Violence and Pan-Islamism since 1979.* Cambridge: Cambridge University Press, 2010.

Hoodbhoy, Pervez. 'Is Pakistan Emulating Saudi Arabia?' *Haq's Musings* [blog] 27 January 2009. <http://www.riazhaq.com/2009/01/is-pakistan-becoming-saudi-arabia.html> Accessed 25 May 2013.

'Iran and Afghanistan.' Institute for the Study of War. <http://www.understandingwar.org/iran-and-afghanistan> Accessed 1 December 2020.

Jalal, Ayesha. 'The Past as Present.' *Pakistan: Beyond the Crisis State.* Ed. Maleeha Lodhi. London: Hurst & Company, 2011. 7-20.

Jenkins, Keith. *Re-thinking History.* New York: Routledge, 1991.

Jinnah, Mohammad Ali. 'Muhammad Ali Jinnah's first Presidential Address to the Constituent Assembly of Pakistan, August 11, 1947.' <http://www.columbia.edu/itc/mealac/pritchett/00islamlinks/txt_jinnah_assembly_1947.html> Accessed 22 May 2020.

Johansson, Ingvar. 'In Defense of the Notion of Truthlikeness.' *Journal for General Philosophy of Science.* Vol. 48, 2017. 59-69.

Kaës, René. Préface, 'Ruptures catastrophiques et travail de la mémoire.' In *Violence d'Etat et psychanalyse.* J. Puget et al. Paris: Dunod, 1989.

Kamal, Soniah. *An Isolated Incident.* New Delhi: Fingerprint, 2014.

Kennedy, John F. 'The Undelivered Speech.' <www.acorn.net/jfkplace/09/fp.back_issues/25th_Issue/jfk_spch.html> Accessed 15 August 2014.

Khan, Nichola. *Mohajir Militancy in Pakistan: Violence and Transformation in the Karachi Conflict.* London and New York: Routledge, 2010.

Khan, Uzma Aslam. *The Miraculous True History of Nomi Ali*. Chennai: Context, 2019.

King, Christopher A., Robert Bienvenu and T. Howard Stone. 'HTS Training and Regulatory Compliance for Conducting Ethically-Based Social Science Research.' *Military Intelligence Professional Bulletin*.US Army, October-December 2011. Vol. 37, No. 4. PB 34-11-4, pages 16-20.

Laas, Olivier. 'Toward Truthlikeness in Historiography.' *European Journal of Pragmatism and American Philosophy*. VIII-2, 2016, Pragmatism and the Writing of History. 1-29.

Lamb, Christopher J., James Douglas Orton, Michael C. Davies and Theodore T. Pikulsky. *Human Terrain Teams: An Organisational Innovation for Sociocultural Knowledge in Irregular Warfare*. Forward by Lieutenant General Michael T. Flynn. Washington DC: The Institute of World Politics Press, 2013.

Lévi-Strauss, Claude. *Conversations with Claude Lévy-Strauss*. Ed. G. Charbonnier. Tr. John Weightman and Doreen Weightman. London: Jonathan Cape, 1969.

Lévi-Strauss, Claude. *Tristes Tropiques*. Tr. John Russell. New York: Atheneum, 1967.

Lewis, Wyndham. *Self Condemned*. (1954). Santa Barbara: Black Sparrow Press, 1983.

Luttwak, Edward. 'Dead End: Counterinsurgency Warfare as Military Malpractice.' *Harper's*. February 2007. 33-42.

Mann, Michael. *The Sources of Social Power*. Vol. I, *A History of Power from the Beginning to A.D. 1760*. Cambridge, UK: Cambridge University Press, 1986.

Mannheim, Karl. 'Das Problem der Generationen.' 1928. In *Wissenssoziologie*. Ed. Kurt H. Wolff. Neuwied: Luchterhand, 1970. 509-565.

Marcel, Jean-Christophe and Laurent Mucchielli. 'Maurice Halbwachs's *mémoire collective*.' In *A Companion to Cultural Memory Studies*. Eds. Astrid Erll and Ansgar Nünning, in collaboration with Sarah B. Young. Berlin and New York: Walter de Gruyter, 2010. 141-149.

McFate, Montgomery and Steve Fondacaro. 'Reflections on the Human Terrain System During the First 4 Years.' *PRISM* 2, no. 4 (2011), pages 63-82. <http://cco.dodlive.mil/files/2014/02/Prism_63-82_McFate-Fondacaro.pdf> Accessed 7 October 2014.

Middleton, David and Steven D. Brown. 'Experience and Memory: Imaginary Futures in the Past.' In *A Companion to Cultural Memory Studies*. Eds. Astrid Erll and Ansgar Nünning, in collaboration with Sarah B. Young. Berlin and New York: Walter de Gruyter, 2010. 241-251.

Mitchell, Peta and Jane Stadler. 'Redrawing the Map: An Interdisciplinary Geocritical Approach to Australian Cultural Narratives.' *Geocritical*

Explorations: Space, Place, and Mapping in Literary and Cultural Studies. Ed. Robert T. Tally Jr. New York: Palgrave Macmillan, 2011. 47-62.

Mohammad-Arif, Aminah. 'The Diversity of Islam.' *A History of Pakistan and its Origins*. Ed. Christophe Jaffrelot. London: Anthem Press, 2004. 223-236.

Morey, Peter and Amina Yaqin. *Framing Muslims: Stereotyping and Representation after 9/11*. Cambridge, MA and London: Harvard UP, 2011.

Moslund, Sten Pultz. 'The Presencing of Place in Literature: Toward an Embodied Topopoetic Mode of Reading.' *Geocritical Explorations: Space, Place, and Mapping in Literary and Cultural Studies*. Ed. Robert T. Tally Jr. New York: Palgrave Macmillan, 2011. 29-43.

Mukayiranga, Speciosa. 'Sentiments de rescapés,' in Catherine Coquio (dir.), *L'Histoire trouée. Négation et témoignage*, Nantes: L'Atalante, 2003. 776-783.

Mwangi, Wambui. 'The Stutter of the Real: Counterfeit Currency and Colonialism in East Africa.' Unpublished manuscript, undated.

Nail, Thomas. *The Figure of the Migrant*. Stanford, CA: Stanford UP, 2015.

Naqvi, H. M. *Home Boy*. New York: Shaye Areheart Books, 2009.

Neumann, Birgit. 'The Literary Representation of Memory.' In *A Companion to Cultural Memory Studies*. Eds. Astrid Erll and Ansgar Nünning, in collaboration with Sarah B. Young. Berlin and New York: Walter de Gruyter, 2010. 333-343.

Nyman, Jopi. *Home, Identity, and Mobility in Contemporary Diasporic Fiction*. Amsterdam and New York: Rodopi, 2009.

Olick, Jeffrey K. 'From Collective Memory to the Sociology of Mnemonic Practices and Products.' In *A Companion to Cultural Memory Studies*. Eds. Astrid Erll and Ansgar Nünning, in collaboration with Sarah B. Young. Berlin and New York: Walter de Gruyter, 2010. 151-161.

Overgaard, Søren. *Wittgenstein and Other Minds: Rethinking Subjectivity and Intersubjectivity with Wittgenstein, Levinas, and Husserl*. Routledge Studies in Twentieth-Century Philosophy. NY: Routledge, 2007.

'Pakistan Denies Reports Saudis Funded Nuclear Program.' *Dawn*. 7 November 2013. <http://www.dawn.com/news/1054796/pakistan-denies-reports-saudis-funded-nuclear-program> Accessed 8 November 2013.

Paracha, Nadeem F. 'Smokers' Corner: Petro Games.' *Dawn*. 24 February 2013. <http://www.dawn.com/news/788269/smokers-corner-petro-games> Accessed 4 April 2013.

Peer, Basharat. *Curfewed Night: A Frontline Memoir of Life, Love and War in Kashmir*. London: Harper Press, 2010.

Pestre, Elise. *La vie psychique des réfugiés*. Paris: Editions Payot & Rivages, 2014.

Philosophy of History After Hayden White. Ed. Robert Doran. London and New York: Bloomsbury, 2013.

Polk, William. *Violent Politics*. New York: Harper Collins, 2007.

Popper, Karl. *Objective Knowledge*. London: Oxford UP, 1972.

Price, David H. *Weaponizing Anthropology*. Petrolia, California: CounterPunch, 2011.

Prieto, Eric. 'Geocriticism, Geopoetics, Geophilosophy, and Beyond.' *Geocritical Explorations: Space, Place, and Mapping in Literary and Cultural Studies*. Ed. Robert T. Tally Jr. New York: Palgrave Macmillan, 2011. 13-27.

Qadeer, Mohammad A. *Pakistan: Social and Cultural Transformations in a Muslim Nation*. London and New York: Routledge, 2006.

Quammen, David. *The Flight of the Iguana: A Sidelong View of Science and Nature*. New York: Scribner, 1998.

Reulecke, Jürgen. 'Generation / Generationality, Generativity, and Memory.' In *A Companion to Cultural Memory Studies*. Eds. Astrid Erll and Ansgar Nünning, in collaboration with Sarah B. Young. Berlin and New York: Walter de Gruyter, 2010. 119-125.

Ricoeur, Paul. *La mémoire, l'histoire, l'oubli*. Paris: Editions du Seuil, 2000.

Rorty, Richard. *Contingency, Irony and Solidarity*. Cambridge: Cambridge UP, 1989.

Roy, Arundhati. *Azadi: Freedom, Fascism, Fiction*. UK: Penguin / Random House, 2020.

Roy, Olivier. 'Islam and Foreign Policy: Central Asia and the Arab-Persian World.' *A History of Pakistan and its Origins*. Ed. Christophe Jaffrelot. London: Anthem Press, 2004. 134-147.

Ruela, Rosa. 'Portugal. Lisbonne, fief de l'Agha Khan.' *Courrier International* (No. 1445 du 12 au 18 juillet 2018), 16.

Sahlins, Marshall. 'The Return of the Event, Again: With Reflections on the Beginnings of the Great Fijian War of 1843 to 1855 between the Kingdoms of Bau and Rewa,' in *Clio in Oceania: Toward a Historical Anthropology*, ed. Aletta Biersack. Pages 37-100. Washington, D.C.: Smithsonian Institution Press, 1991.

Said, Edward. 'Reflections on Exile.' *Reflections on Exile and Other Essays*. Convergences: Inventories of the Present—Book 26. Cambridge, MA: Harvard UP, 2002. 137-149.

Salami, Ismail. 'Carnage of Shia Muslims in Pakistan.' *Press TV*. 6 September 2012. <http://www.presstv.ir/detail/2012/09/05/260017/genocide-of-shia-muslims-in-pakistan/> Accessed 4 June 2013.

Saunders, Max. 'Life-Writing, Cultural Memory, and Literary Studies.' In *A Companion to Cultural Memory Studies.* Eds. Astrid Erll and Ansgar Nünning, in collaboration with Sarah B. Young. Berlin and New York: Walter de Gruyter, 2010. 321-331.

Sewell, William H. Jr. *Logics of History: Social Theory and Social Transformation.* Chicago and London: The University of Chicago Press, 2005.

Shamsie, Kamila. *In the City by the Sea.* London; New York: Bloomsbury, 1998.

Shamsie, Kamila. 'Offence: The Muslim Case,' in *Manifestos for the 21st Century.* London, New York and Calcutta: Seagull Books, 2009.

Shamsie, Kamila. 'In Pakistan, there's no Answer to Terror.' 19 February 2013. <http://www.theguardian.com/commentisfree/2013/feb/19/pakistan-terror-murder-shias-baluchistan> Accessed 14 February 2014.

Shamsie, Muneeza. *Hybrid Tapestries: The Development of Pakistani Literature in English.* Karachi: Oxford UP, 2017.

Sharma, Aradhana. *Logics of Empowerment: Development, Gender, and Governance in Neoliberal India.* Minneapolis: University of Minnesota Press, 2008.

Sheen, Farrukh. 'Women and Ethnic Identity: Case of MQM,' in *Locating the Self: perspectives on Women and Multiple Identities,* eds. Nighat Saeed Khan, Rubina Saigol and Afiya Shehrbano Zia. Lahore: ASR Publications, 1994. 205-214.

Siddique, Osama. *Snuffing Out the Moon.* Haryana, India: Hamish Hamilton/Penguin, 2017.

Skocpol, Theda. *States and Social Revolutions: A Comparative Study of France, Russia, and China.* Cambridge: Cambridge University Press, 1979.

Southgate, Beverley. *History meets Fiction.* Edinburgh Gate, UK: Pearson Longman, 2009.

Steinmetz, Horst. 'History in Fiction—History as Fiction: On the Relations between Literature and History in the Nineteenth and Twentieth Centuries,' in *Narrative Turns and Minor Genres in Postmodernism,* eds. Theo d'Haen and Hans Bertens. Amsterdam: Rodopi, 1995. 81-103.

Sugiyama, Satoshi. 'Doors for Refugees Close as Displaced Population Soars, U.N. Says.' *New York Times* (19 June 2018). <https://www.nytimes.com/2018/06/19/world/middleeast/displaced-un-report.html> Accessed 9 July 2018.

Tally, Robert T. 'Geocriticism and Classic American Literature.' English Department Faculty Publications, paper 14, Texas State University, 2008. <http://ecommons.txstate.edu/englfacp/14>

Tolentino, Jia. 'A Novel About Refugees that Feels Instantly Canonical.' *The New Yorker* (10 March 2017). <https://www.newyorker.com/culture/jia-tolentino/a-novel-about-refugees-that-feels-instantly-canonical> Accessed 9 July 2018.

Understand al-Qur'an Academy. 'And the answer is …Al-Wakeel!' 9 March 2019 <https://understandquran.com/answer-al-wakeel.html>

Waheed, Mirza. *The Collaborator*. London: Penguin Books, 2011.

Walberg, Eric. 'Heart of Darkness: Princess Patricia and the Taliban.' *CounterPunch*. 4 June 2008. <http://tesa.leb.net/walberg06042008.html> Accessed 10 October 2014.

Wallerstein, Immanuel. *The Modern World-System*. Vol. I, *Capitalist Agriculture and the Origins of the Capitalist World Economy in the Sixteenth Century*. New York: 111Academic Press, 1974.

Westphal, Bertrand. *Geocriticism: Real and Fictional Spaces*. New York: Palgrave Macmillan, 2011. Originally published in French as *La Géocritique: Réel, fiction, espace*. Paris: Minuit, 2007.

Westphal, Bertrand. 'Forward.' *Geocritical Explorations: Space, Place, and Mapping in Literary and Cultural Studies*. Ed. Robert T. Tally Jr. New York: Palgrave Macmillan, 2011. ix-xv.

White, Hayden. *The Fiction of Narrative: Essays on History, Literature, and Theory 1957-2007*. Ed. and Intro. by Robert Doran. Baltimore: Johns Hopkins University Press, 2010.

Wittgenstein, Ludwig. *Philosophical Investigations*. Hoboken, NJ: Wiley-Blackwell, 2009.

Yingzi, Tan. 'Yellow River Dams on Verge of Collapse.' *China Daily*. 19 June 2009. <www.chinadaily.com.cn/china/2009-06/19/content_8301942.htm> Accessed 25 February 2014.

Zakaria, Rafia. *The Upstairs Wife: An Intimate History of Pakistan*. Boston: Beacon Press, 2015.

Copyright Acknowledgements

The author and publisher would like to thank the following for permission to reproduce copyright material:

PART 1

Chapter 1
'Traumatic Experience, Crisis of Survival and Healing: Interconnected Itineraries/Histories in Soniah Kamal's *An Isolated Incident*.' *Itineraires/Itineraries*. Les Indes Savantes, forthcoming, https://hal.archives-ouvertes.fr/hal-02425818

Chapter 2
'"Now" and "Then": Mirza Waheed's *The Collaborator* and the Contested History of a Place." Ege University, *Literature, Narrative and Trauma*. Edited by Aylin Atilla, David Waterman and Carlos A. Sanz Mingo. ISBN: 978-605-338-261-4, pp. 119–126. Comité de lecture.

PART 2

Chapter 3
'Migration, Exclusion and the Enemy Within: Personal and Political Displacement in Rafia Zakaria's *The Upstairs Wife*.' Ege University, forthcoming.

Chapter 5
'Neoliberalism, Water Scarcity, and Commonwealth: Mohsin Hamid's *How to Get Filthy Rich in Rising Asia*.' *Uncommon Wealths in Postcolonial Fiction*. Cross/Cultures 201. Eds. Helga Ramsey-Kurz and Melissa Kennedy. Leiden and Boston; Brill/Rodopi (2018), pp. 125–137. Comité de lecture.

PART 3

Chapter 6
'Saudi Wahhabi Imperialism in Pakistan: History, Legacy, Contemporary Representations and Debates.' Mykolas Romeris University, Vilnius, Lithuania. *Societal Studies* 6.2 (2014), pp. 242–258. ISSN: 2029-2244. Comité de lecture

Chapter 7
'Mapping the Human Terrain: Cultural Understanding as Military Strategy in Nadeem Aslam's *The Wasted Vigil*.' *Interactions*, Ege University Press, Vol. 29, No. 1-2, Spring/Fall 2020, pp. 147–155. ISSN 1300-574-X. Comité de lecture.

PART 4

Chapter 9
'*Exit West*: The Making of a World.' *Sociétés en mutation: Culture(s) en mouvement dans les espaces littoraux et urbains*. © Cambridge Scholars Publishing, 2020. Edited by Vincent Mariet, Muthia Chandra, Letyzia Taufani, Martine Raibaud and David Waterman. ISBN (10): 1-5275-5452-X. ISBN (13): 978-1-5275-5452-8, pp. 97–105. Comité de lecture.

Chapter 10
'Snuffing Out the Moon: Kino/Bio Politics, Movement and the State of Exception.' *Commonwealth Essays and Studies—Exception* 43.1 (2020), https://journals.openedition.org/ces/4048.

Index

A

Aazadi, 48, 50
Afghanistan, 1, 7, 8, 16, 17, 66, 73, 74, 77, 78, 85, 86-89, 90, 91, 93, 95
Agamben, Giorgio, 121, 123, 124, 125, 127, 132, 133
Ali, Mehrunnisa, 76
Altounian, Janine, 14-19, 20, 24
Andaman Islands, 8, 96-98, 101-103, 107
Appadurai, Arjun, 115, 118, 119
Arendt, Hannah, 113-117, 119
Aslam, Nadeem, 8, 82, 86, 138

B

Badruddin, Asad, 84
Ballard, Roger, 38
Bauman, Zygmunt, 43
Benjamin, Walter, 127, 128
Bergson, Henri, 47, 52
Beyerstein, Lindsay, 92
Bhutto, Benazir, 6, 37, 40, 41, 43
Bhutto, Zulfikar Ali, 75, 76, 80
Bienvenu, Robert, 95
Bobin, Fréderic, 83
Brown, Steven D., 47, 56
Butt, Nadia, 13-15
Butterfield, Herbert, 38

C

Casey, Edward, 30
Cheah, Pheng, 112-119
Chellaney, Brahma, 61-63, 66, 67, 68
Chill, Steve, 86
China, 7, 29, 83
CIA, 8, 74, 82, 86, 87, 89, 90, 91, 93
Colonial, 8, 88, 102, 117
Cultural memory, 6, 45-49, 51-57

D

Dalley, Hamish, 26, 33, 98
Dalrymple, William, 101
Damrosch, David, 111
Doležel, Lubomír, 97, 104
Doran, Robert, 2
Dufour, Dany-Robert, 19, 20

E

Eswaran, Mukesh, 68
Event, 1, 4, 6, 7, 14, 224, 27, 28, 33, 40, 46, 47, 50, 52, 53, 55, 56, 57, 68, 83, 88, 97, 98, 99, 104, 106, 122, 124, 125, 134-136, 138, 139
Exclusion, 6, 37, 40, 41, 42, 44, 121
Exile, 37, 41, 97, 101-107, 122, 124, 128, 129, 130, 132

Experience, 3, 5, 6, 15-17, 19, 23, 25, 26, 33, 38, 43, 45-49, 50-52, 56, 57, 79, 95, 99, 101, 102, 103, 113, 116, 117, 138

F

Flusser, Vilém, 55
Fondacaro, Steve, 88
Forte, Maximilian, 86
Foucault, Michel, 32, 121, 123
Fradinger, Moira, 42, 121
freedom fighter, 5, 13, 14, 16, 18, 19, 20, 21, 23, 25, 29, 30, 32
Freud, Sigmund, 18, 51
Friedrich, Carl J., 127

G

Gaborieau, Marc, 75
Gayer, Laurent, 37
Generation, 6, 7, 14, 15, 19, 23, 33, 41, 46, 47, 49, 50, 51, 53, 57, 58, 59, 61, 80, 81, 101, 115, 118
Genocide, 14, 78, 83,
geocritical, 25, 29, 31,
geopolitics, 29
Gledhill, John, 69
Gonzalez, Roberto J., 87
Gupta, Akhil, 59, 60, 61, 64, 65, 67-69

H

Halbwachs, Maurice, 47, 48, 49, 52
Hamid, Mohsin, 7, 8, 59, 60-64, 66-69, 80, 111, 112, 114-119, 120, 138
Hamilton, Sharon R., 86
Hanif, Mohammed, 81
Hegghammer, Thomas, 74
Historiography, 3, 8, 97, 100, 104-106

Hoodbhoy, Pervez, 79
Hudood Ordinances, 6, 39, 41, 43, 77
human terrain, 8, 85, 86-89, 91-95

I

Identity, 25, 26, 31, 32, 48, 55, 56, 79, 80, 115, 123, 138
Imagination, 3, 4, 98, 100
Immigrant, 38, 43, 44, 138
Indus Valley, 9, 73, 81, 120, 131, 138
Islam, 1, 40, 54, 55, 73, 75-79, 80-82, 84

J

Jalal, Ayesha, 75
Jenkins, Keith, 96
Jinnah, Mohammad Ali, 74, 75
Johansson, Ingvar, 104

K

Kaës, René, 18, 24
Kamal, Soniah, 4, 13, 14, 19, 22, 23, 137
Kashmir, 1, 4, 5, 6, 7, 13-16, 22, 24-27, 29, 30, 31, 33, 45, 47, 50, 51, 53-57, 137, 138
Kennedy, John F., 92
Khan, Nichola, 39, 41
Khan, Uzma Aslam, 8, 96-99, 100, 102-107, 138
King, Christopher A., 95
Kinopolitics, 121, 122, 124, 128, 130, 132
Kotwal, Ashok, 68

L

Laas, Olivier, 97, 104
Lamb, Christopher J., 85, 87-89, 90, 91, 95
Landscape, 26, 27, 28, 29, 30, 32, 85, 138

Lévi-Strauss, Claude, 69
Lewis, Wyndham, 22
Line of Control, 5, 25, 29, 57
Luttwak, Edward, 94

M

Mann, Michael, 136, 137, 139
Mannheim, Karl, 47
Mapping, 8, 31, 85, 87, 89, 91
Marcel, Jean-Christophe, 47, 48, 49
McFate, Montgomery, 88
Middleton, David, 47, 56
Migration, 1, 6, 8, 9, 37, 38, 40, 111, 114, 115, 118, 120, 129, 132, 134, 138, 139
Militant, 20, 29, 30, 31, 32, 46, 49, 83
Minority, 76, 117
Mitchell, Peta, 31
Mohammad-Arif, Aminah, 75, 76
Morey, Peter, 43
Moslund, Sten Pultz, 30, 31
Mucchielli, Laurent, 47, 49
Muhajir, 39
Mukayiranga, Speciosa, 15
Mwangi, Wambui, 63

N

Nail, Thomas, 120-128, 130, 131, 132
Naqvi, H. M., 81
Natality, 113, 114
Neoliberal, 7, 59, 60, 138
Neumann, Birgit, 52, 55-57
Newcomer, 9, 38, 39, 113, 116, 118, 119, 134, 139
Nomad, 29, 124
Nyman, Jopi, 13, 14, 16, 22

O

Olick, Jeffrey K., 49
Orton, James Douglas, 92, 93

P

Paracha, Nadeem F., 83
Partition, 1, 6, 7, 26, 31, 37, 38, 53, 77, 104, 134, 138
Peer, Basharat, 6, 45-48, 50-57, 138
Pestre, Elise, 15, 18, 19, 23
Plurality, 102, 113, 114, 116, 117, 137
Polk, William, 91
Polygamy, 6, 41, 44
Popper, Karl, 104
Postcolonial, 26, 33, 112, 113, 117, 118
Poverty, 59, 60, 61, 62, 67
Price, David H., 86
Prieto, Eric, 25, 27

Q

Qadeer, Mohammad A., 77
Quammen, David, 33

R

Ramaswami, Bharat, 68
Reulecke, Jürgen, 46
Ricoeur, Paul, 3, 4
Rorty, Richard, 97
Roy, Arundhati, 5, 6
Roy, Olivier, 77
Ruela, Rosa, 119

S

Sahlins, Marshall, 135
Said, Edward, 101-105
Salami, Ismail, 78
Saudi Arabia, 7, 54, 73-79, 80-84
Saunders, Max, 45, 52
Sewell, William H. Jr., 1, 134-137
Shamsie, Kamila, 39, 41, 75, 76, 80, 82
Shamsie, Muneeza, 1
Sharma, Aradhana, 59
Sheen, Farrukh, 42
Shia, 7, 74, 76, 78, 82, 83
Siddique, Osama, 9, 120-126, 128, 131, 133, 138
Skocpol, Theda, 135
Southgate, Beverley, 20-22, 24, 38
Stadler, Jane, 31
Steinmetz, Horst, 38, 46
Stone, T. Howard, 95
Storytelling, 96, 113, 115, 116
Sufi, 32, 54, 55, 73, 79
Sugiyama, Satoshi, 111

T

Taliban, 77
Tally, Robert T., 31
Tolentino, Jia, 111
Torture, 5, 14, 16, 18, 47, 50, 92, 93, 94
Totalitarian, 9, 119, 129, 137
trauma, 5, 15, 26, 51, 57
traumatic, 4, 5, 6, 7, 13, 15, 16, 17, 19, 23, 26, 33, 49, 57, 137, 138

U

United States, 4, 74, 77, 82
usable past, 6, 55

W

Waheed, Mirza, 4, 25, 137,
Wahhabi, 73-78, 83
Wallerstein, Immanuel, 135, 136
War, 1, 5, 6, 7, 8, 27, 28, 39, 41, 46, 47, 49, 50, 54, 57, 60, 64, 66, 74, 75, 77, 79, 80, 82, 87, 89, 91, 97, 98, 102, 103, 106, 120, 124, 130, 134, 138
wealth, 59, 60, 61, 65, 66, 68,
Westphal, Bertrand, 28
White, Hayden, 2, 3
Wittgenstein, Ludwig, 100

Y

Yaqin, Amina, 43
Yingzi, Tang, 148

Z

Zakaria, Rafia, 6, 37, 137
Ziaul Haq, 7, 37, 39, 41, 73–6, 79, 80, 81, 82, 84